MINISTRY WITH YOUNG COUPLES

MINISTRY
WITH
YOUNG
COUPLES

A Pastor's Planbook

Douglas W. Johnson

Abingdon Press / Nashville

MINISTRY WITH YOUNG COUPLES
A Pastor's Planbook

3/91

Copyright © 1985 by Abingdon Press

This book is printed on acid-free paper.

Library of Congress Cataloging in Publication Data

JOHNSON, DOUGLAS W., 1934–
  Ministry with young couples.
  Bibliography: p.
  1. Church work with young adults. I. Title.
BV4446.J64   1985   259   85-4050

ISBN 0-687-27043-X (pbk.: alk. paper)

MANUFACTURED BY THE PARTHENON PRESS AT
NASHVILLE, TENNESSEE, UNITED STATES OF AMERICA

C.1

Contents

Preface..7

Preface

M ost difficulties in this world can be traced to the fact
that everyone doesn't think and act as we do. Once
they get smart and listen to us, the world is going to be a lot
better off.

How many times have we heard or felt those words! But
God's children aren't the same. They're diverse. Therefore
congregations are different and each attracts particular
types of people. This book accepts diversity. Nevertheless,
when dealing with young couples, no matter the type of
congregation or hue of its membership, certain information
and procedures seem to be universal. Those universals
are stressed in this book, even though much leeway for
churches with divergent needs is suggested.

Young couples, defined as being between twenty and
thirty-five, are crucial to the life of the church. Young

couples are the future. Yet they must interact with older people (defined in this book as those over forty-five) to make that future useful. It's true that they need what older people have to offer. Conversely, their fresh insights and new ways of approaching old problems can give new meaning to older people in their commitment to Christ.

May your young couples' ministry be effective.

DOUGLAS W. JOHNSON
Ridgewood, New Jersey

CHAPTER ONE

Who Are They?

Young couples between twenty and thirty-five years of age live in the apartment across the hall." "They're in the house down the street." "They are my kids." "They are my grandchildren." "They are a weird group." "They are the fabric of society."

"Young couples are rebellious." "They are dedicated to changing everything around here." "If they don't like what we do, they can go somewhere else." "They like music that's loud." "They don't believe in disciplining their kids." "They want the good things in life for the least amount of effort."

These random descriptions of young couples over twenty and under thirty-five are accurate, even though biased by the experiences of the reporters. Every couple that has lived through these ages knows, if recall is truthful, the pleasant and distasteful epithets above could have fit them, as well as those now classified as young couples. By human design, these are years of transition and building. They are times of growing and testing. They are years full of hope and ambition. Positive expectations have not been blunted by long-term responsibility, which comes with growing families and midterm careers.

While only a few of the more caustic descriptions may apply, most young couples would admit to being a bit rebellious. And no wonder! They have reached an age when they are expected to become independent. They have to rebel. They must have their own identity. The comfortable era when they were protected as young singles by their parents must change. They have to grow up as couples!

People who reach twenty years of age are thrown out of the parental home, if not in fact, at least in psychological terms. They are sent away to college, to military service, or to jobs. While they may be invited to continue to live with the parents, sometime before their late twenties they are expected to make a break and establish their own homes.

Despite their occasional short tempers, young couples need each other and older people. They need as much help as they can get, as long as the assistance is listening and making suggestions rather than prescribing a course of action. They need help because young couples face five significant decisions. The choices they make will determine the direction of their lives for decades.

The five very important decisions young couples make are: (1) what their careers or jobs will be; (2) where they are going to live; (3) whether to have children and, if yes, how many; (4) how they are going to establish their independence from their parental families while maintaining contact; and (5) whether they are going to continue with their present partner.

These choices are open to review. Several of them must be affirmed or revised regularly, especially those about careers or jobs, partners, and independence from parental families.

10

The need for remaking these choices is a constant reminder of the insecurity of a young couple's life.

In addition to constant insecurity, young couples face other stresses. For instance, their decisions are made in bunches rather than serially. Young couples do not have the luxury of adjusting to the consequences of one decision before they are required to make another. Several decisions, each of them life changing, may have to be made at the same time. In a sense, young couples are learning to survive in a cauldron of opposite emotions, any one of which may dissolve their partnerships. No wonder young couples can be described in so many ways. They present several facets to parents, friends, peers, and colleagues.

Parents can be a major source of stress to the couple. Parental advice is not based on the same experiences and social setting and may not be useful. Thus, advice and counsel received from older adults must be recalculated to fit current circumstances.

The availability of contraceptive devices and a more tolerant view of sexual activity have created a contemporary world view contrary to the one that governed their parents' early married years. These changes have prompted a significant increase in the number of unmarried couples. Another difference is the prevalence of drug use among young people now.

The examples cited do not imply sexual activity always occurs prior to or without marriage, or that drug use is an invention of the current group of young couples. The difference is the openness and widespread involvement as opposed to more covert indulgence of former generations.

A powerful force currently affecting young couples is the women's movement. This movement is especially salient for its effect on exposing long-standing inequities in jobs, wages, treatment before the law, and family, especially alimony, wife beating, and battered children. These issues have been addressed by previous generations but have not had the widespread or systematic attention that they have now.

The effects of this attention are difficult to comprehend, but subtle changes are evident in roles within the home. Publicly, the effects are noted as day-care and pre-kindergarten centers become more available and babysitting becomes a profession. In the changes created by adjusting sex roles, young couples make internal family commitments, which may involve reconceptualizing more traditional models. The process of relearning roles can add to the normal tension that is part of the decision making required of the age.

While young couples are living in a world with somewhat different stresses than did their parents, their values are not counter.[1] What make young couples a difficult group for the church to involve in programs are their selective attitudes. They have grown up in an era emphasizing self-fulfillment and the need to get the best possible. This attitude was instilled in them by their parents!

One effect of this attitude is that young couples don't come to church out of habit or because there isn't anything else to do on Sunday morning. They come because they believe the church has something worthwhile to offer. And if *this* church has something better than *that* church, they'll go here. They look below the surface. They are sophisticated church shoppers!

As a group, they are better educated, more affluent, have a better fix on who they are and what they want to do, and are more at ease in a technological society than previous generations. When these attributes are put beside the tough decisions they are making, young couples are a group of people who are exciting to be with and hard to work with.

Decision Points

The five decisions identified previously are representative of stages in a young couple's life together. The first stage begins by becoming independent of each set of parents. This usually starts when marriage plans are made. This is probably the most significant independent judgment, and the first, made by a young person. Parental influences may be detected during dating, but the final choice of a mate is made by each partner as an independent decision. This may come before or after individual choices of careers are made by the potential partners.

A career or job choice, another stage for a couple, is usually amenable to redirection or revision by a mate. In fact, careers and jobs may be changed or aborted by mutual consent after marriage. For example, both partners may be working, but an advancement opportunity for one may mean a move limiting the work time or making it impossible for the other to continue working. The new opportunity, which enhances the life potential of the couple, may dictate a career change or at least a revision for one partner. Or, accepting a new job may mean, as some young couples have discovered, establishing a commuting marriage. This occurs when the partners live in different places because of work assignments and commute to a common home weekly or twice a week.

Choosing where to live, another decision point, is related to career and independence from the parental families. Becoming a couple generally means finding a place to live other than in either parental home. Some young couples make this choice without being married. They choose a partner and live together but must choose where to reside.

Quite often a place to live is mandated by where they work and what they can afford. In a few cases, young couples are subsidized in their housing. Parents of one of the partners may purchase a home for the couple as an investment or as a gift. This is especially the case when the parents seek investment opportunities and feel real estate is viable. However, relatively few young couples are offered this option.

Deciding on a place to live brings with it several smaller but related choices. Choosing whether to purchase furniture, considering the amount of commuting time and its ease, assessing recreational and educational opportunities, and being comfortable with the prevalent life-style of the proposed living area are other factors that influence where a couple lives.

Determining where to live is quite important because the young couple is establishing a pattern for their later life. Although an average young couple may move several times, for many couples, their first choice will be their home for years. This may not be their initial expectation, but the costs of moving and purchasing or renting other housing may prohibit changes later.

These three decisions affecting independence, job, and residence generally occur during the first few years of marriage or before most partners reach thirty years of age. The average age for marriage is under twenty-five years for both males and females. The experience level of young couples is not great, given the kinds of choices they must make during their first few years of marriage.

Finalizing independence from parents is not completed by the age of twenty-five for most. Vestiges of dependence may linger for years beyond. However, the crucial first steps have been taken and will not be reversed, even though a divorce may ensue and one of the partners returns to the parental home for a time.

Revising a career or job choice may occur immediately upon marriage, although it more likely comes during the ages of twenty-five to thirty. A few years of experience in a job are needed before a company or a person may want to invest money in changing jobs. When one is asked to take a new assignment or a partner chooses a new job, the impact of the choice affects both partners. Oftentimes the new job includes more responsibilities and may involve working in another location. Even if the new workplace is within commuting distance, the commute requires revision in the couple's planning. Some changes in household roles also may occur.

During the ages of twenty-five to thirty, decisions about children are made. This is a fundamental choice and greatly affects life patterns of the couple from then onward. They no longer will be a couple but a threesome or a foursome or whatever. Their responsibilities will increase manyfold. As they assume parenthood, they will ask for assistance with their new roles, creating fellowship or neighborhood groups for people their own age and in similar circumstances.[2]

A continuing decision for the young couple is whether to remain together, with the most crucial time for this decision coming between the ages of thirty and thirty-five. Many couples divorce within two years after marriage, but the average divorce comes after seven years. This statistic makes the early thirties a significant time for married couples.

The decision to remain a couple must be made regardless of the type of couple. Most eventually marry. This means heterosexual couples who live together will be faced with a decision sometime in their late twenties or early thirties whether to be married or to break up, and most will marry.

Types of Couples

The three general types of couples are: unmarried, married, and remarried. Single people who are divorced and have children to raise may, and often do, remarry. However, unless they have been involved in a program with a young couples' group prior to their divorce, it is unlikely they will be participants in a couples' ministry while they are single. Their needs may be better met by short-term involvement in a single adult ministry.[3]

1. *Unmarried Couples*

The most prevalent form of unmarried couple is a man and a woman living together. Nowadays, these couples may be young or old. I note in passing that an increasing number of couples with partners over thirty-five are living together without marriage as a result of economic pressures and longevity.

The number of unmarried young couples living together has increased dramatically since 1970, representing a change in living arrangements from other experiences in this century.[4] However, historic common law indicates men and women have been living together without marrying for centuries. The incidence of such cohabitation in recent years has risen primarily because of relaxed social attitudes and independence on the part of females.[5] Unmarried couples tend to concentrate in urban centers, college communities, and areas where such living arrangements are not questioned.

The church's concern should not be whether a couple is married. Its need is to understand that these couples have the same emotions, problems, and opportunities as those who are married. In fact, many unmarried couples, because they are not asked about their marital status, are assumed to be married by their neighbors and friends. Interrogating a couple about their marital state should not be a prerequisite for their participation in a couples' ministry.

Another form of unmarried couples is homosexual or lesbian in nature. Despite increased attention in recent years, such couples are not new.[6] However, their presence is more evident in some localities than in others. Considering the preference of homosexual couples to be in a supporting and compatible environment, many live in enclaves within large cities. Their nonwork activities, because their life patterns are different from those of other couples, focus on organizations amenable to issues and concerns related to their life-style.[7]

Homosexual or lesbian couples are productive members of ministries when prejudice toward their sexual orientation is curtailed. Their needs and concerns as couples are similar to those of other couples, including married couples.

In fact, those with long-term mates are faced with most of the major decisions of heterosexual couples.

2. *Married Couples*

This is the form of young couple encountered in most congregations, yet there is not an abundance of them in the church. The younger couples, consisting of those between twenty and twenty-five, are hardest to involve. Often, they were not reached as young single adults. Consequently, they have broken ties with the church and will need to be rewon as couples. Helping young couples forge a strong relationship with the church as they begin their life together is critical since this is the time when they most need the support and fellowship of a church-based group like themselves.

Although married couples, as a form, are the most prevalent, there are two subcategories within it. The two types are those with children and those with no children. The latter may or may not eventually have children. Statistics suggest few will remain childless.

Childbearing may occur at any time for a married couple. However, women are now putting off childbearing until their mid- to late twenties. This means partners under twenty-seven have different interests and needs than those who are between about twenty-eight and thirty-five years of age. The distinction between the groups tends to be made around children. Suggested ages are averages and vary from community to community. Adjustments needed with the advent of a child or children are substantial. As a result couples are separated into interest groups focusing on children or the lack of them. This distinction should have a direct bearing on church programming.

3. *Remarried Couples*

Divorce influences the attitudes of couples even before marriage. Marriage contracts are evidence of the importance

17

of divorce as an option. Maintaining a marriage is not now, nor has it ever been, easy. Increased equity for women, especially when this includes income equality, has made divorce an attractive option to a poor marriage. The potential to exercise this option can increase the strength of marriage over the long term. Evidence in one long-term study suggests divorce has actually strengthened couples' bonds rather than weakened the institution of marriage.[8]

Most divorced persons remarry after a time.[9] Remarried couples must face the same decisions (usually for a second time for at least one partner) that every other couple confronts. Therefore, they need the same type of program as other young couples. A program for couples should address issues and needs *for them* rather than selecting a standardized program for couples.

Statistical Information

A few facts from statistical data about young couples can assist us in understanding them:[10]

About 90 percent of American adults will marry during their lifetime. However, in 1982, about a third of those twenty to twenty-four, two-thirds of those twenty-five to twenty-nine, and three-fourths of those thirty to thirty-four were married. These figures point to the differences in types of ministry needed by specific age groups. At least half of all young couples who marry will include one partner beyond the age of twenty-five.

The average age at first marriage was about twenty-two for females and twenty-four for males in 1982. These ages were older than the comparable twenty and twenty-three years for females and males in 1960. The average age at remarriage has gotten younger during the past fifteen years. In 1965 the man remarried at forty while the woman was thirty-five. In 1982 the median age at remarriage was thirty-two for the woman and thirty-five for the man. These data support the contention that young couples are more likely than older folks to terminate their marriages.

In most unmarried couples, the female partner is usually under thirty-five years of age. In some cases, these liaisons are a transitional stage between divorce and marriage for many persons. Males in unmarried couples tend to be somewhat older than their female partners.

The number of children per family is about two, with most women bearing children after age twenty-five. Slightly more than half the families had children of their own under eighteen years of age living with them in 1982. This was lower than the 56 percent with their own children under eighteen at home in 1970. Family size has dwindled even as the number of children involved in divorce and in single-parent families has increased significantly.

The greatest increase in working mothers since 1970 has been in women who have children under six. Nearly half of these young mothers were in the labor force in 1982. The trend seems to be for women in young couples (under thirty-five) to continue to work after marriage.[11]

The income earned by wives is less than that earned by their husbands, but this inequitable situation will be reversed, perhaps due to court decisions. Income from wives tends to increase the mode of living of the couple.[12]

Since 1978 more females than males have been enrolled in colleges. Education levels are equal in young families, which means sophistication levels are about the same for both partners.[13]

These statistics provide useful information, but the problem with such data is that it doesn't fit any given community well. The data should be used as a background against which to compare a local situation. For example, young couples now have a higher level of education than previous generations. While this statistic may be true, it doesn't matter in locations where young couples do not speak standard English, where education is not valued, or where school systems are inferior.

A more accurate assessment of young couples, which may or may not show up in educational measurements, can be made by asking: How sophisticated are they? What is their degree of self-reliance as a couple? What are their lifetime expectations? Answers to these questions will provide most of the data needed to gauge the types of programs needed by the couples.

Income levels, especially as they relate to young couples, must be understood in terms of job opportunities for females. For instance, females now outnumber males in colleges. A part of this has to do with an increase in chances for them to pursue careers requiring college training. A woman who was a secretary in a previous generation needed a limited education, but now executive positions for females are a possibility. Women who want these positions generally have to secure college degrees. In this way increases in educational levels are related to other, mostly economic, factors. In communities where economic advancement for women is not a possibility, educational attainment may not be an incentive.

Data tell us more wives, including those with preschool children, are working now than previously. A longitudinal study revealed such change occurred among women of the middle class.[14] It is quite common for both partners near the poverty level or in the early stages of marriage to be working. The shift from homemaker to career person has occurred among women of affluence. These women are attending college and vying for male-oriented jobs, such as doctors, lawyers, ministers. In addition, women are also plumbers, carpenters, pilots, transport drivers, and the like.

It is accurate to say a higher percentage of wives work now than earlier, but in some communities the statistic is inappropriate. Ethnic communities know it is often the female whose income provides a firm foundation for the family. Couples living in economically depressed areas are aware of the continued importance of working wives. In these areas, general statistics just don't tell the whole story.

20

Two-income couples are an increasing force. Yet the cost of both persons working is high if the the jobs call for commuting, special clothing, regular continuing education courses, and child care. Much of one person's wages, at least, is absorbed by the need to pay for services necessary to allow both to work and to pay the increased taxes that are a result of additional income. These costs may negate most of what one partner makes. However, two-income couples are able to withstand economic hardship better than couples in which only one partner works. If one person's job is lost, the couple can survive on the remaining income. They will not do as well as before, but they can survive better than former generations.

Statistics about couples, therefore, must be related to local experiences. A ministry shouldn't be based on general information about society. It has to be developed on the basis of experiences of people in your neighborhood and those who can be touched by your congregation. Understanding their level of sophistication, their expectation of life, and their economic situation is more important than quoting the latest census data. A couples' ministry is specific to an area and a group. Any data used to create and maintain a young couples' ministry must relate to the potential participants.

How Important Are They?

A pastor friend of mine, when asked how important young couples were to the church, answered like this: "They are to the church what the chicken and the egg are to creation. They are the source as well as the sustenance of its life."

I thought about this for awhile and concluded he had a worthwhile analogy. Young couples are the source of children on whom the future of the church depends. At the same time, young couples can provide enthusiasm, new ideas, and energy to get things done. If this is what he meant, the pastor was on target with his philosophical response.

Those people twenty through thirty-four are part of the baby-boom generation that is rewriting social barometers in the United States. They made up 30 percent of the population in 1982, compared to 22 percent in 1960. In addition to being the largest group in the U.S., they are affluent, outspoken, open about sex, willing to acknowledge mistakes and try again (divorce and entrepreneurship are two examples), and interested in the church's message. They are competitive, concerned about health and self-improvement, and like to travel and relax. They want to be associated with success.

Many are moving into nonurban areas and trying nontraditional occupations. They understand security, but many seem to be willing to forego it when it conflicts with their desire to be in command of their lives. Some are involved with the technological revolution that is reshaping the industrial sphere of society; others are involved in communications industries. All are innovative and risk takers.

It is hard to know how to measure the importance of a generation as talented and as hard to please as this. Conversely, they are not asking to be pleased. They seem to prefer a challenge as long as there is recognition of their effort and accomplishments. They are willing to do whatever is necessary if they are trained, supported, and rewarded.

These young couples will be the backbone of the church's membership and the source of its giving, leaders, and participants for the next three to four decades. Many in number, these couples will have many children who could vitalize church schools. If the church does a good job of programming for them now, the future of the church will be bright. The opposite is true if the church fails them.

CHAPTER TWO

Attitudes and Values

We got married just after we graduated from college. Then we packed up and moved to California. Our reason was for me to complete graduate school, but our real motive was to have time to get to know each other without our parents' interference." The young man looked across the table at his friend. "Do you know what I mean?"

The friend nodded and replied. "That surely was a long way to go for independence! But I know what you mean. It's taken us these past four years to be able to make a choice without one of our parents telling us what to do."

"It's not that we don't want our parents to care. We do. In fact, they visited us at least once a year when we were in California. That's quite a trip from southern Ohio. But they made it. We were just as happy when they left." The two friends laughed.

"It's so hard for parents to believe we can grow up and make our own decisions! But we have a life of our own the same as they have their own life."

These two midwestern young men are talking like people Gail Sheehy interviewed for her book *Passages*.[1] They are young professionals in their late twenties who have been married for fewer than five years. As is true of many contemporary young couples, the wives work full time. One couple has a young child, and the other couple is expecting a child within two months. These husbands and wives are part of the church's future, both because of who they are as couples and the fact that they are bearing children who will be the next generation of churchgoers.

Their attitude toward parents may seem harsh, and it may be disquieting to the parents. If this happens, it is unfortunate. Yet, to the parents, suddenly they have lost a son or daughter. The parents undergo a separation trauma when a son or daughter leaves home to set up one of his or her own. Fortunately, time allows healing to occur, and parents are able to confront separation from their child.

On the other hand, the young couple, although feeling the change, generally is not overcome by separation from parents. Their choice to live as a young couple means they are adding a great deal more complexity to their lives than they anticipated. In one sense, their adjustment to each other is more difficult to handle than the parents' feeling of separation, because young couples have no previous similar experiences to help them. Each must meld his or her life with the life of another person. The adjustments required are as traumatic for them as is separation for the parents.

Young couples are able to cope by concentrating on themselves. This intensive inward focus is a trait common to young couples. Their primary goal is establishing a meaningful partnership with a chosen mate, and they want this relationship to have intimacy.[2] Intimacy, however, must not smother either partner's personal identity or goals. In addition, the relationship has to help both of them, or they will opt for divorce or separation. Young married couples do not feel bound to continue in a poor marriage any more than unmarried couples want to continue living together.[3] Their concern is to find a way to balance personal and corporate needs for security and independence.

The perennial struggle of humans to be safe while remaining free to pursue personal hopes and dreams is an urgent occupation of young couples. Not only are they working at becoming adults and finding a niche for their talents and efforts in a new world; they are doing it in partnership with someone else. The assignment is awesome, but their attitudes are practical and optimistic. They believe they have chosen mates who can assist them in accomplishing their dreams. If the partnership doesn't work out, however, they will call the marriage or relationship quits and begin again.

A significant aspect of a couple's immediate task in living together is discovering who they are and who their mate is. As with most others, young couples select mates according to an imaginary prototype. If they wish to remain married, or together if they are unmarried, they each must move from the fictionalized to the real person with whom they are living. In the process of grinding down the idealized image to reality, the couple must develop a supportive means of readjusting their individual pictures and expectations of the other. This adjustment period, usually occurring before age thirty, is a difficult time since young couples are required to handle an idyllic adventure with another person while being pummeled by the realistic demands of a job. It is surprising to young couples, but not to parents or other observers, the strains they feel with each other.[4]

One of the positive things going for them is a value base. Values are transmitted early and are subconscious guides to behavior over an entire life. While it is relatively easy to change attitudes, it is very difficult to radically adjust values.[5] A preponderance of social data about young couples is attitude-related, not value-oriented and does not reveal their values. Yet, the data should not be discounted since people act on the basis of current attitudes. For instance, young couples are attracted to a church because of its current leadership, not the long-term value a church has in working with neighborhood people.

The internal interplay between attitudes and values never stops. Every experience can result in a revision of an attitude and a test of a value. Indeed, when people become couples, underlying values become very important in understanding why they are acting a certain way. Three types of values are especially noticeable and show up as characteristic attitudes in young couples.

One characteristic of young couples is their *pragmatism*. For example, divorce is a pragmatic decision, even though an underlying value of both partners may be maintaining a strong marriage. The value, strong marriage, cannot be upheld due to weaknesses created by one or both mates' inability to function as a full partner in the marriage. Since both want (or value) a strong marriage and both feel their relationship cannot be strengthened, they decide to divorce. While pain comes from their pragmatic choice, it is temporary. The value of having a happy and satisfying marriage can be more compelling than negative reactions from peers or parents to getting a divorce.

Another characteristic of young couples is the *determination* to forge their own life pattern. This is the gist of this chapter's opening conversation between the two young men. They, along with their wives, wanted opportunities to choose, to succeed, and to fail on their own. They didn't say they were overwhelmed by the multiplicity of decisions or the struggles they encountered. Their focus was on having a chance to try! How can they test their wings if they never use them?

A third characteristic of young couples is *sophistication*. Their experiences since childhood have included understanding sex, expressing themselves through music and dance, self-improvement, travel, and technology. Their perception of world affairs has been shaped by television and commentators as often as by journalists. They have had money to purchase "wants" as well as "needs." Many worked while attending school and know the meaning of disciplined effort. Their concept of self-gratification is egalitarian in that both males and females are willing to pursue their feelings rather than live by a double standard. They do not hesitate to criticize elders for actions or values inconsistent with what they profess.

These three characteristics, pragmatism, determination to do for themselves, and sophistication, separate this generation from previous ones. They have lived entire lives within an affluent and indulging society. Yet, their inclination is to be tough on issues and policies that might make the future difficult. This extends to such concerns as the environment, gun control, nuclear armaments, and toxic chemicals. While they appear to be selfish in protesting current policies and conditions, their values are future-oriented. They want a good life, no doubt, but they wish to extend better conditions to their offspring than was true of their childhood surroundings.

It is little wonder, given these inclinations, that older adults have difficulty comprehending the direction of young couples. Young couples act from a different base and understanding of life than older people do. As a result, conflict, covert or overt, is a common companion of meetings or activities bringing older and younger couples together. Underlying values may be the same, but the manner in which they are lived out is quite different. The divergence can be traced back to the completely different beginnings of the generations. None of us outgrows our childhood. We tend to see the world through those eyes for a lifetime. In this sense, older people, especially those over forty-five, have a hard time understanding the thinking of the young.

Formidable though the task, it is incumbent upon both groups to understand each other and to work together. The church is composed of all generations and is not the exclusive territory of one age or status group. Since change (though not the exclusive prerogative of young persons) is most often instigated because of pressures they put on older persons, both parties must identify attitudes that propel young couples. These attitudes will affect everything young couples do and will determine the extent to which young couples participate in the church or in a special program designed for them.

Identifying feelings and ideas does not mean all of them are acceptable. Just because young couples are motivated by their own perceived values and long-term interests in a certain direction doesn't mean the church has to indulge their whims (such as a week-night club for young mothers or a drama club for those under forty). A congregation is a disciplined community of believers. As such it must weigh inclinations and ideas, no matter how innovative or attractive, according to their effects on the congregation's mission and ministry. The ideas most beneficial to the entire church will be adopted in the long run.

Pinpointing attitudes common among young couples is one step in detailing a ministry for and with them that enhances the outreach of a church. Some of the more important attitudes we will examine deal with work, sex, money, discipline, and the church.

Work

"The most important thing about my job is feeling I do something worthwhile. I can't stand boring, dead-end jobs."

A fellow worker nodded and added, "When you see how your part helps the whole, it makes you feel good."

An office worker, at break, was talking to a friend. "Sometimes I feel trapped by machines. There are days, like today, when I am in front of the word-processor nearly the whole time. I can't be a person. It makes me feel like an extension of the machine."

"I'm certainly glad to hear you say that! I thought I was the only one who felt like that!"

A young couple who decided to quit their jobs and start a business in a small town were asked why they made the jump. After a brief silence, the woman responded. "We felt that the work we were doing was important and useful, but somehow it wasn't fulfilling. I was one lawyer among many in a firm, and my husband was a C.P.A. with another big firm. We probably would have moved up the ladder in time. Money wasn't the reason, either. Our combined salaries were better than we will make for quite a while in this business."

The husband broke in. "We looked at ourselves and said, 'So what?' We had a lot of things but we never saw each other; we didn't share life goals; we didn't work together. We want to be something together."

She picked up the story. "We talked about it for a few months and started looking around. We found this. It makes us creative and keeps us together. The kind of business we own has let us move into an environment where we can work at our own pace and gives us time to do things other than work."

In a different interview, a young couple is asked about their decision for the husband to stay home with the child while the wife works. The wife answers, "It wasn't much of a decision for us. I had the job with the most promise for advancement. We felt we didn't need any more income. Bill has skills he can use at home like writing and doing odd jobs. He has a degree in social work and can use that if the need arises. When we moved here, we agreed to test this arrangement for a few years. So far, it has worked out well."

Her husband agreed. "I like the opportunity to be at home. It has upset our parents some, and in this community it isn't expected that a man will take care of a young child. For example, I'm never included in neighborhood social events during the day because they are for women only. But I am giving our child a father image very early in life.

Only a few children have such an image. We think that's important."

This small sampling gives a clue to the diversity of attitudes about work held by young couples. Work is important. It provides opportunities for self-expression; it rewards people with money; and it wraps couples in protective benefits such as insurance and pensions. Work, on the other hand, can be stressful; it may separate couples; it creates tensions among couples; and it can cause divorce. Young couples are aware of the two-edged sword of work. Their awareness is evident in decisions relating to the kinds of work they do, their willingness to give up security and to strike out on their own, their experimentation with changes in who will be the main breadwinner, and their insistence that work aid them in their growth as people and as a couple.

None of these are new attitudes. Any innovative idea young couples have toward work is grounded in a feeling that they have the ability to make it no matter what the circumstances. They have been raised in an affluent environment. They know how to work the system in order to help themselves through very difficult times.[6] For example, they are not hesitant to apply for food stamps. Nor are they adverse to using public clinics and visiting nurses. They don't recall the stigmas associated with accepting "relief," which may have prohibited their parents from considering tapping such resources in earlier days. Indeed, such resources may not have been available to previous generations.

Another factor in their attitudes toward work is that both partners may have—or may want—to work.[7] More than half of the wives of young married couples work, although many hold part-time jobs.[8] If necessary, the couples can shift the main breadwinner role. The wife can work full time and the husband will look for a part-time job.

In several parts of the nation where companies have closed, this has occurred. The family's income will not be as high as it was when the husband worked full time, but there will be money enough to live. This recognition of shared responsibility has not been so important in the previous generation when husbands were thought to be primary providers.[9]

Independence may be an apt description of the primary attitude of young couples toward work. They know its importance, but for them work must be put into a holistic perspective toward life.

Young couples work hard and are ambitious. But somehow, their addiction to work doesn't seem as pronounced as was the yoke carried by some former generations. As a result, the young couple today appears flexible in what they want to do and to be over the long term. They view work as a means to other ends rather than as an end in itself.

On the other hand, the work ethic does not seem to have diminished.[10] Young couples like to feel what they do makes a difference. They are not often bored at work and most of the time feel they do their jobs well. Conversely, nearly half feel they would prefer to change jobs in the future.

With at least half of the wives in married couples employed, new occupations have been created. Day-care centers, pre-kindergarten schools, and full-time babysitters have sprung up catering to couples where both parents work. Companies include pregnancy leaves as part of the personnel policies. In some situations, a new father receives a brief time off work with pay to assist his wife. None of these practices or centers were as widespread in other decades.

Available data, therefore, suggest work continues to be a strong value for young couples. Any change in emphasis between current and previous practices focuses on the reasons young couples have for working.

"A job is my way of getting what we need." A young wife who works part time as a waitress tells why she is working. "Bill was working two jobs, but he was so tired and tense all the time it wasn't worth it. I persuaded him to quit one job and took this waitress position. It isn't much, but I work during the day. We have a friend take care of our three-year-old. I make enough to pay my friend and make up for Bill's second job. We have free evenings now and can live a little."

Her motivation for working is not self-fulfillment in her job. She wants a meaningful relationship with her husband. Since he couldn't meet the financial needs of the family by himself, she stepped in to help. In her way, she is helping them both find self-fulfillment by outside work. A job, to her and to many young couples, is strictly a means to a much more productive end.

Work is a necessity but it involves both, not just one, of the partners. This attitude toward work is important to remember when dealing with young couples.

Sex

Contraceptives and sex education have combined to change sex from a procreative activity to a means of intimacy and self-expression. Although it is difficult if not impossible to document, it is likely the use of birth control pills has been a significant factor in the increased number of unmarried couples living together during the past decade or so. Fear of unwanted pregnancy has been curtailed and, for those who become pregnant, the availability of legal abortions has made living together as unmarried couples less threatening.

Homosexuality has come into public view in an unprecedented manner. During the past decade, political activism on behalf of homosexuals has emphasized job discrimination.[11] Homosexual couples are trying to find acceptance in the larger society by suggesting sexual preference is a private, not a moral, issue. This argument has divided the populace. Discrimination, accusations of immorality, and countercharges about limiting freedom of sexual expression will continue to hamper dialogues between heterosexual and homosexual groups. Nevertheless, openness about sex has made homosexuals a visible entity and, in some instances, a force in communities.

Sex continues to be a commodity used to sell almost every product to the general public. It is used freely in movies, novels, and television to induce people as viewers or buyers. Sexual activity is now open and explicit as opposed to being more covert and suggestive in earlier times. Manuals suggest sex can be a sport engaged in by persons interested in hedonism. Most television shows display sex as an activity that can be separated from intimate feelings and love.

Yet, most young couples think of sex as a form of intimacy.[12] They are not convinced sex should be an indiscriminate activity undertaken freely and with no consequences. They want sex to be a part of their relationships to the extent it enhances their intimacy as a couple.[13] This attitude implies that overt experiments with free sex among couples is no longer acceptable. Sex among couples appears to be indicative of deeper feelings than promiscuous sex requires. This mood change in society may have been strengthened by attitudes and certainly by practices of young couples.

Even though sex is regarded as a normal function of a couple, young couples have not forgotten this is the way children are conceived. They are taking advantage of birth control methods to limit unwanted pregnancies. Relatively few of them are opting for no children. Parenthood is coming at later years for couples, which may make them more ready to handle the myriad complications new parents find with children.

Just as likely, these new parents, although in their late twenties or early thirties, will demand more assistance as they try to adjust a comfortable life pattern for two people into a pattern accommodating three or more. They will have had experience in developing a career and starting to build a couple. They have no experience in handling a career or job along with maintaining an intimate relationship with a spouse while meeting the basic needs of a child or children. Sex, for the couple, becomes different.[14] They will need to redefine intimacy and once more establish familial sexual patterns.

Sex for new parents is a critical issue. To help them through troubled times, a supportive group for young couples with small children can be of great help. A church program for young couples ought to help them express and creatively cope with their sexual feelings both before and after childbirth, because both partners will feel differently about sex after their first child. Also there is a time of abstinence males may not fully understand. A new mother uses most of her energy to care for the child and doesn't have much left to engage in sex.

Money

"Who ever has enough money? We afford everything we need and a lot of what we want. We have dreams about a new home, travel, and things like that. But we get along with what we have."

"We have chosen a limited life-style. We want to get back to basics. We use a wood stove to heat the house and have good insulation. We use public transit whenever possible and have our own vegetable garden. These are symbolic things to most people, but to us they emphasize our commitment to a particular way of life."

"We have more than we need. Sometimes we feel guilty, especially after we see a television report on hunger or poverty. However, we aren't willing to make drastic changes in the way we function as a family. We save and are careful of resources. We teach the children to be frugal. But we aren't paupers and don't intend to be."

"We both work and with two children under five, we have to make a lot of compromises. We negotiate our vacations, take turns staying home when a child is sick, and regularly evaluate our babysitter. There's stress but nothing big. We like our jobs and have no qualms about letting our children be with a babysitter. The time we have for them is higher quality than if one of us stayed at home all day. As far as the money is concerned, that's almost secondary to feeling productive and useful through our jobs."

"Money is our ticket to dreams. We both work just so we can have things and go places. We save a little but not much. If a child comes, both of us will probably keep working. We like the good things in life, and working is the only way we can get them."

Money is a very important commodity in this society. It really is a ticket to dreams. Money also provides the necessities for living. Without money, a young couple would have few opportunities to find a meaningful future. Given its importance, it isn't surprising to learn that family arguments over money are frequent and intense.

Although legal tender is the primary means for getting ahead, acquiring wants, and providing a cushion for the future in this society, there are many divergent views about money. Some feel the more they keep the better off they will be, while others understand money to be a means for establishing and maintaining a life-style. Both viewpoints are valid. A commodity is important to the well-being of a society and can be used as an end in itself. For instance, gold can be hoarded, made into beautiful jewelry, or molded into a statue for a public museum.

How money is used reflects a life pattern. The so-called jet set squanders money in displaying how much they have. A middle-class couple invests money in a house and neighborhood as a measure of stability. An affluent couple has an investment strategy, perhaps two homes, and a regular schedule of vacations and travel. A poverty-level couple tries to keep the family together and survive in a continually hostile environment in which jobs are hard to come by, difficult to keep, and pay minimum wages. In each situation, access to money predicts the life-style. Society gives people status by the way they spend as well as the method they have of getting money.

Members of young couples who are under twenty-five are at their lowest earning points. They are getting started in jobs and must take what is available. Although not totally inexperienced in handling money, they don't have as much cash or as many assets to handle as older couples, even those in their late twenties and early thirties. The lessons they learn early about money will help young couples in the future.

One of the most important things they learn is to use credit. They quickly realize that their needs, when they first marry, cannot be satisfied by the money they have or make. Some couples, however, postpone marriage and accumulate such items as furniture, appliances, and cars with the use of credit. Most of these loans can be paid off in three to five years. Perhaps being able to get married with the necessities paid for is one of the reasons many couples wait until their late twenties. Also, their incomes will be higher the longer they work and the more skills they develop.[15]

Economic security for young couples is not so important as liking a job.[16] Feature articles in newspapers and magazines have focused on young couples who quit a well-paying position to go to a not so well-paying one in a totally different environment. Their reason for change is self-fulfillment as a couple. Economic security is not as important.

This doesn't mean young couples are less able to fend for themselves.[17] They often begin life with more things than previous generations. They may not start life as a couple with a great deal of money but neither do they commence debt-ridden. In addition, a working wife adds to a married couple's income an average of slightly more than four thousand dollars. This amount is enough to raise the family into the next income level and often moves them from subsistence to better living standards.[19]

Money is recognized as a necessary part of life by young couples. They may not have the same compulsive need to accumulate money or possessions as did older generations. This is demonstrated by a young couple's willingness to change jobs as they look for a satisfying career or job. They may be unwilling to work overtime because they value other aspects of life more than money. They may invest and save for retirement as means of insuring the continuation of their life pattern well into the future.

A measure of their attitude about maintaining a particular life pattern is evidenced by a survey reported in *USA Today* (April 11, 1984). The kind of house most often purchased by young couples in 1983 was an older house. The mortgage was so high it required two incomes to pay it. Couples were buying houses like the ones they grew up in. There may be gentrification (rebuilding older urban neighborhoods) in some cities by affluent, professional couples, but the majority of young couples want to spend their money in ways that support life-styles similar to that of their parents.

Because they have been used to money their entire lives, young couples and their attitudes toward money may appear more casual than the attitudes of older people. This should not lead observers to believe young couples are unaware of money's usefulness. Nor are they unsophisticated about investment, pensions, credit, and taxes. They may need help in each of these areas but so do older people. Younger couples, because they have listened to those older, are better able at a younger age to treat money as a means rather than as an end.

Discipline

By observing how willing young couples are to postpone immediate gratification in order to enjoy pleasures at a later time, we can understand a measure of their discipline. Young persons are getting married later than earlier generations did. Perhaps some of these people may have lived together or with someone else for a time without marriage.

Another way that young couples show how disciplined they are is by not having a child soon after marriage. This is a rather typical attitude. Of course it is true that waiting to establish a family has been assisted by improved birth control measures.

Young couples, as a group, appear to put restrictions on themselves. They place demanding requirements on their relationships, even those not married. For those unmarried couples, older people see their live-in arrangements as a basic inability to face the demands of marriage. What these older people with such an attitude fail to comprehend is how difficult it is to maintain a stable relationship, a relationship often maintained solely because of the will of the partners. Unmarried couples, unlike married counterparts, have no legal obligation to remain together. So discipline is an important ingredient in keeping them together.

Another example of discipline of young couples is the high percentage that work. Even though the woman must contend with traditional roles, she works more often now than in the past.[20] Young couples are a disciplined and thoughtful group of people. Just because they express their wills differently than previous generations does not mean they lack discipline.

A different type of discipline relates to those couples who have children. In the late seventies, a study of young parents showed a fourth of them being strict (using old-fashioned methods of discipline), a fourth being permissive, and slightly more than half being between these in exerting discipline on their children. When the three types of parents were divided by age, more of those under thirty-five were permissive than those older.[21]

Permissive parents tended to be better educated and more affluent than the other two categories of parents.

Strict parents were less well off and least secure as parents. The temperate parents were more inclined to use discipline than were permissive parents but held to many traditional values relating to family ties.

Each of these types of parents will be found in a congregation among young couples. Their primary distinctions will be their world view about themselves and their children. The permissive will tend to be more liberal, while the strict will tend to be very conservative. The majority of parents will be temperate.

Trying to get across the value of hard work, religion, saving money, and family ties was important to a majority of the parents in this study.[22] They impressed upon children the importance of duty before pleasure and the wrongness of prejudice.[23] The values they cling to and want to pass on to their children are similar to those of older generations. The main difference between young and older couples is their backgrounds. Discipline is as important nowadays as before, but it is discussed in terms of its effect upon the long-term development of children.

Young couples are disciplined as individuals, as families, and with regard to their children. Variations in discipline tend to be related to education and affluence. When their methods of discipline disagree with the predominant view of their elders in a community or church, young couples are branded as being undisciplined. Their problem is not discipline but who defines discipline.

Church

Religion remains crucial to the people in the U.S.A.[24] In spite of trends that point to decreasing attendance at worship services and fewer members in certain denominations, people display strong religiosity. A majority of adults claims allegiance to some form of Christianity.[25]

Religious commitment appears to increase with age. For example, adults under thirty are less likely to be attenders at worship or be as religiously oriented as older people.[26] On the other hand, young couples with children are inclined to seek some form of religious instruction at least for their children.[27] A sample of comments from young couples illustrates diversity in their attitudes about the church.

"We haven't been active in church because we've been too busy. I don't remember the last time I've even attended church. But with Jill getting ready to go to nursery school, we feel she needs grounding in some ultimates. We're not prepared to talk to her about God or death or anything like that. So we brought her to church."

"The church has been a powerful force for both of us since we were young. We have been active and feel our children will benefit from it as much as we have. Faith is the only solid thing in life. We look to the church to give it to us and to our children."

"A few of our friends have suggested we go to church. They belong to a group that seems to have a good time. We haven't felt the urge or need. Maybe one of these days we'll go try it out. Meanwhile, we are content with life as it is now."

Young couples are certain they can conquer every obstacle in life. Their optimism is a product of youth and affluence. They don't believe human fallibility includes them. Even in situations where tragedy befalls a member of their family or a friend, they have a notion it couldn't happen to them. This attitude changes as years and experiences accumulate.

Their attitudes toward church tend to be guided by (1) their perceptions of the ability and integrity of the pastor and (2) their feeling of acceptance by a peer group within the church. This shouldn't be surprising since these are the two major factors affecting attendance and church affiliation.[28] Unfortunately for many congregations, the number of young couples is so small that they are considered nuisances rather than people needing a ministry.

Young couples bring to church a sense of their own insecurity, an urgency to do things now rather than carefully consider alternatives, demands for quality church school for their children, and requests for opportunities to influence the program and direction of the congregation. It is little wonder that a new group aggressively trying to change a church will be considered a disruptive influence. Patience among older people is worn thin by demanding attitudes of young couples. Consternation in congregations often can be traced to outright rejection by young couples of comfortable methods.

Abrasive is the word some congregations use to describe young couples. The word is an accurate description, but it fails to catch the undertone of need and insecurity with which young couples approach the church. They may have been out of its sphere of influence for several years and are coming back with notions about its activities that remain fixed on childhood experiences. They must undergo training and updating before they are caught up with what the church is really doing now. Meanwhile, questioning and disparagement about current church activities is a normal stage for young couples.

The young couples with the most education and who are more affluent will be difficult to handle. Working mothers are not dealt with successfully by very many congregations, because attitudes about child care and personal self-fulfillment may not be understood by older adults. Young couples, indeed, can create ferment. Yet, their interests and needs are similar to those of older individuals. And, older couples can be a great help to younger colleagues because of "having been there" before.

In spite of brashness, young couples are a needed asset to any congregation. Once their long-term concerns are identified, these people are just like the rest of us.

CHAPTER THREE

Issues
Concerning
Young Couples
❧✿❧

W hat's my concern? Right now it's making enough to pay my bills. If you mean in the next few years, it's doing something worthwhile. Another concern is trying to keep my relationship with my partner fresh and meaningful."

"Raising our children is our greatest concern. How to balance their and our needs so none of us gets too crimped seems to be the heart of the issue. Money and what it can buy is always a concern."

"Working toward my next advancement is very important to me and, I think, to my family. Right now I'm about two years away from a big promotion. It's going to take all my concentration and energy to get ahead. The family is going to suffer a little. We've discussed this thoroughly and believe the promotion will justify our sacrifices."

"Our biggest worry is keeping together. We both work and have to travel for work. We're apart much of the time. It's almost like we're strangers when we do get home on the same day. We have to start all over on each occasion. We're not sure what the future will bring."

Social commentators frequently describe the current age in terms of rapid and widespread social change. They focus primarily on technology in making this assessment. Those who rely on other factors such as divorce and the increase in single-person families tend to use census materials or trend data as though they were totally accurate. Writers in the popular press, newspapers, and magazines interpret history as being not longer than thirty years.

Such approaches in social analysis cannot accurately describe a continually changing complex society like ours. A careful analysis of social change deals with continuity factors. One enlightening search for causes underlying current political and social issues stresses the theory that current issues are repercussions created by specific historical decisions.[1] This continuity stresses the makeup of social environments. Given the need people have to retain a set of values throughout life, young couples are beneficiaries and products of earlier generations. Data from one careful multi-generation study suggest young couples today face life-changing decisions similar to those that couples throughout the years have confronted.[2]

Indeed, issues of consequence to young couples are the same as those of most other adults. This will be clear to older people who study the habits and attitudes of young couples. Differences between older and younger couples are found in the way they deal with themselves and their surroundings. The way we confront life is determined from our early lives.

In fact, the primary criteria determining how young couples are going to handle the decisions they face and the results of choices they make are rooted in their upbringing. Young couples, especially those with children, are trying to

43

pass on values in harmony with those they inherited from their parents.[3] However, their social situation has changed considerably since they were young.

Three recently published studies deal with the social environment and the issues that young couples are concerned with. However, these are not the only sources for gaining a perspective on young couples' perceptions of their world. Feature articles in newspapers and magazines, and stories on television regularly describe issues facing young couples. The three studies cited, however, extrapolate the social environment and its inherent issues into the future whose foundations are in issues and concerns described by the studies. The composite world view, including an emphasis on personal self-fulfillment, meaningful work, personal relationships, and the worth of each individual, is presented by these studies and dominates our environment today.

John Naisbitt's contention in *Megatrends* is that society is changing to a personal from an impersonal, hierarchical form.[4] Young people, including young couples who are acting on their carefully calculated long-term plans, are shaping a social atmosphere in which emphasis is shifting from merely doing to doing things well. They want rewards for their efforts, but their main concern is finding fulfillment in what they do and become.

A stress on meaningful family and work life is posited by Alvin Toffler in *The Third Wave*.[5] He sees young adults carrying out values they learned from parents. These values are self-fulfillment, quality of life, concern for the environment, raising children in an atmosphere in which they can achieve personal development, and the proper use of technology.[6] Smallness, or at least reduced size, will become the norm for companies and work groups, allowing individuals to excel and have a peer/support group simultaneously.

Thomas Peters and Robert Waterman in *In Search of Excellence*[7] examined companies and discovered accents on personal relationships, people treated as individuals with worth, peer work groups, and values expressed through work and products. The authors concluded that when company leaders encourage workers to be people who want to find self-fulfillment and worth through their employ, the company and its employees benefit. Excellence is not a product of bigness but of values expressed by the corporate leadership and internalized by the entire workforce.

These three studies plus the sociological study of Middletown give us a framework within which we can visualize issues concerning young couples. It is true that today's issues are similar to those handled by earlier generations. However, because each generation lives in a different social setting, the methods for dealing with issues by today's young couples will be different from those of previous groups.

Today's young couples are more sophisticated, more affluent, and better educated than any former generation. As a result, they are more pragmatic, more realistic, and more willing to be in conflict than older folks. They are outspoken, testy, and challenging. At the same time, they are sentimental and are seeking inner direction for their lives.

These attributes and attitudes are hard to accept by many older persons who are rooted in churches. Many of these older adults try to maintain the status quo; consequently, they resist change. Young couples want to make a difference and are impatient with the slowness of change in some churches. When they are met head-on by older persons who resist change, young couples, since they have limited loyalty to any particular congregation, will look for another one where their ideas and presence will find better reception.

Since they are mobile, they are not bound to go to a church near their home. Therefore, if this church doesn't provide for them and their children, they will look elsewhere. Young couples are active and aggressive. They expect others to be the same. They do not expect to get their way all the time, but they do want to make a difference. Continually thwarting them will drive them away quickly.

Young couples, in spite of wanting to be on their own and independent, are very peer-oriented. They are concerned about what others think of them. Their children must fit in and do those things children of their peers are doing. They want to keep a bit ahead of the peers but not so far ahead in either achievement or status that they lose position in the group. They are reluctant to share innermost feelings but are adept at playing the game of "tell me about your feelings." They are articulate and inner-directed but usually when it is to their advantage.

None of these are negative factors in themselves. The description identifies sophistication within a group. Of course, not every young couple fits a broad description. Enough young couples can be included in these descriptions to say that young couples, as a group, act pretty much like this.

Considering the kind of people who are young couples, it shouldn't startle a congregation desiring to minister effectively to young couples when its efforts are rebuffed. Young couples may not seem to want to have a special program just for them. On the other hand, a careful review of community-sponsored programs and activities indicates they want and need several types of programs. The most important thing they need, however, is understanding. One part of understanding comes from analyzing some of their issues.

Quality of Life

A young man, being interviewed for a job, kept asking the question, "Will I have the freedom to pursue some of my own interests?" The interviewer didn't know how to respond so he just nodded. The young man took the job with a feeling he had alerted the interviewer to an

46

agreement about how the job was to be filled. The young man was going to work for the company, but while doing his best for the organization, he would fulfill his personal needs. He saw no conflict in meeting personal as well as accomplishing corporate goals.

A young couple was talking to a real estate agent about purchasing a home. The agent asked, "What are your basic desires as a family?"

The young couple looked at her and were silent for a time. Finally, the wife spoke. "We want a community where the children can get to the center of town by themselves, where there *is* a center to the town, where they can participate in school activities without being driven by auto, and where we are protected from a lot of traffic." She looked at the agent. "Of course, we have the normal needs of a four-person family."

The agent smiled and nodded. "I knew about the four people in the family. I didn't know what kind of life you expected to live in this community."

Quality of life is decided not by external trappings but by how well the needs of people are met. For couples, quality of life includes satisfaction of internal as well as external needs. In general, the characteristics of a couple with a quality relationship are: being compatible with each other, able to discuss problems and opportunities openly and easily, and able to arrive at mutually satisfactory decisions about problems or opportunities. To enhance their external quality of life, they would want to live in an atmosphere that encourages their self-development, and relate to groups and organizations having stimulating and supportive programs. Relatively few young couples live in such an ideal setting. They settle for the best life they can afford either in money or in psychic energy. Indeed, quality in life is defined differently by each young couple.

Young couples, as a group, are searching for a setting in which they can find excitement, challenge, and security. The search generally is conditioned by limits and compromises.

The tension between the search and the compromises affects a couple's quality of life. Each couple can pursue challenges they choose so long as they are willing to fail. They must have the freedom to choose and not succeed. This is difficult for them to accept because of their inner optimism and the dependence they place on peer relations. Security, they soon discover, is illusive no matter what age the couple happens to be.

The elements shaping the quality of life include living place, number and type of relationships, physical and emotional surroundings, opportunities for personal accomplishments, and rewards. Each of these is very important to young couples, and often they are not put together as a means for developing the quality of life. When young couples compare notes on these items, they test what they have with what others possess. Their tabulation of pluses and minuses will give them a quality of life score, even though they may think in terms of status.

Young couples don't stand around with calculators and tote up averages. Yet, their memories and minds work overtime as they compare their life advantages with the advantages of others. Life is a social event. Young couples must learn how to live it together. In the process, they search for internal pictures of fulfillment. Those pictures—ideals—are parts of their image of a hoped-for quality in life.

One of the major differences between these younger people and older people is the ability to articulate their ideals. Young couples, because of their educations, seem to be more adept at planning than older persons. They are willing to think carefully about life's opportunities and problems. In fact, they use planning as a way of disciplining themselves. They consider several angles to a proposition before committing themselves, and this slowness and seeming indecisiveness may frustrate older generations. This is unfortunate because older people have been trying to get younger people to listen to them and use their knowledge since the beginning of humanity. Now, when young people think for themselves, older people are frustrated.

Planning helps young couples create lives with quality. The three social analyses cited previously emphasize that people under thirty-five view social settings and values critically. They are unwilling to accept at face value the enticements of work, passivity in entertainment, or self-congratulations by social organizations. They want specifics, particularly self-fulfillment and worth, from their efforts and involvement. They expect something back from their efforts with organizations, including the church. Congregations find an attitude like this hard to deal with, insisting that programs and activities adequate for people in past generations are sufficient for today.

A generation interested in improving life's quality is not going to be impressed with "life as usual" programming. They want the best that can be provided within their limitations of money and time. Quality has not been a hallmark of many congregations. Perhaps this is a reason churches find the insistence of young couples on quality of life both frightening and frustrating.

Personal Gratification

"We're going to travel for a week. We know we shouldn't spend the money, but life's too short to spend working all the time. We're going to enjoy it while we can."

The ad on television shows a product and a model clinches the sale by saying, "It costs more, but I'm worth it."

A mother is talking about her daughter and son-in-law. "They decided to postpone having a child and are taking a year off to go to Europe to school. They said they wanted to have a good time before settling down with a family. I don't understand it. When I was twenty-seven, we had a home of our own, two children, and a steady income. This generation baffles me."

The mother doesn't realize what she is saying. She has, through hard work, discipline, and deferred gratification, given her children a better economic and educational start in life than she had. She wants them to enjoy life while they're young; she's told them as much. Now she wonders at their attitude and action. This mother, like those of many young couples, forgets that she and other mothers hold firmly to the work ethic. They also forget that the young couples are doing exactly what they, as parents, have suggested. Parents learned that self-gratification ought to be satisfied during youth, not in old age. Young couples have taken this advice seriously.

Young couples, by observing older couples, have learned the more obvious side effects of an unbridled work ethic. They believe it gave to their parents' generation a mentality unwilling to admit to prejudice, a temperament unable to acknowledge the importance of luck, and a life pattern minimizing satisfying personal relationships. As children who grew up under the pressures of the work ethic, they rebelled—became the flower children and have selectively chosen pieces of that ethic to guide their lives. One thing they have chosen is to have a good time while they are earning a living and creating as a couple. They were taught this value by parents who only wished they could do the same.

Older folks demonstrated by their self-denial and subsequent unhappiness the need for personal gratification. Young people got this message and because their parents have provided them opportunities, are incorporating enjoyment and pleasure into their lives. They are not willing to work for some far off nebulous goal. They are realistic in establishing a life model and working toward it. It contains personal pleasure even though the model also stresses discipline and hard work.

Future Security

"Who doesn't want security? I'd like to know I'll be able to afford everything I want and need. I'd like to know I'll always have a job. I'd like to know my family will stay together. But life isn't secure. We plan, but we're living one day at a time. Future security is a dream."

The young woman was completing her introductory session for the new job. "Would you please repeat the information about insurance and pension? I think I got it, but I want to make certain."

A young man was talking to his father. "My broker said this company is going to make it big. I don't usually believe brokers, but I went to the library and did some checking on my own. He's right. Maybe you can put some money on it and make a few dollars."

Security is defined as freedom from danger or risk. When it comes to security, young couples are a study of diametrically opposing forces. They want security at the same time they want the challenge of risks. They are as selective of the types of security they want as they are of most other aspects of life. They want to be protected from health hazards. They want insurance so they don't have to worry if some illness or accident befalls them. They want a good job, a place to live, and a satisfying relationship. These are security.

By the same token, they seem not to be so concerned about being shielded from risks. They will leave a job if it doesn't give them a satisfying approach to life. They will stop a relationship if they feel cheated or bored. They will divorce a partner if they can't work out a compatible life pattern. They will criticize traditions even when those habits could provide comfort and solace. Young couples prefer to choose the form of security that fits their life goals.

The most preferred form of future security is a guarantee that their future will be no worse than their present life. Consequently, they are quite interested in pension benefits. These are a form of such a guarantee. They go to school and enroll in continuing education courses after graduation, which is a type of insurance against job loss. In addition, they feel secure because they are willing to move to follow jobs. They will ask parents for help. These are various types of security all pointing to a future that is relatively risk-free in terms of personal comfort.

They look for, and find, security within themselves and their capabilities. They are not hesitant to tap their parents for financial assistance. They are willing to have parents initiate contacts on their behalf. These are forms of security that cannot be measured in financial terms.

On the other hand, they are not prone to seek risk-free lives. Indeed, risks are part of being young and a couple. Young couples are optimistically confident of their capability to overcome most obstacles. Perhaps the most noticeable attribute of this generation is their self-confidence. This may be a reason their primary security requirement is that they may continue living as they are accustomed.

While their immediate attention is upon personal security, over the long term they are concerned about other forms of danger. Pollution, especially from chemicals and nuclear energy, is a constant source of concern. Young couples tend to be more aware of dangers from chemical imbalances, acid rain, and other pollutants than are older folks. They are interested in protecting their bodies from such dangers. In this sense, they want the environment clean because they are concerned about their future security.

Environment

Environment includes not only the earth, sky, and water resources but social situations as well. Both kinds of environment receive much attention from young couples in very direct ways. They lead protests against nuclear power reactors because of the dangers posed for themselves and their children. They petition governments to clean up chemical wastes. At the same time, they believe in letting the public know about child molesting, rape, and spouse abuse in order to point out problems endemic to social settings.

They want an environment in which they can feel protected and relatively free to fulfill their life hopes.

Of course, not every young couple is on a protest march or a picket line. Many are content to allow companies and organizations dictate policies and ignore problems within families because internal family difficulties are personal. Yet, young couples are involved in campaigns to clean up longstanding environmental problems. Young couples also are challenging the way people have treated child abuse, rape, physical and emotional disability, and other social problems.

In one sense, young couples are agitators. They can't seem to allow situations to remain as they are. They insist on change, especially if someone in their family is affected by the situation that needs changing. Emphasizing the need for good quality in life—these couples are unafraid of organizations, corporations, or established traditions. This makes them pesky foes. Their training and background make them formidable opponents as well. They know how to work the systems of which they are a part. When they want a good environment, they get involved in making it better.

A young parent with a child may be pictured among those protesting trains carrying nuclear wastes across their state. Another young parent may be one of several lawyers representing class action suits against a corporation or state that discriminates against women by not paying them as much as men for comparable jobs. A young couple may be the most vocal critics of the local city council's decision to widen a street. The parents' contention is that increased traffic will endanger children and add to pollutants. These are young couples who want change. They are willing to risk ridicule and the resulting effect on their security as they fight for physical and social improvements in their world. In these respects, they are different from their parents, who were more willing to endure discomfort because they lacked the self-confidence needed to take on entrenched practices.

Young couples are not going to save the world. That's not their mission. They want a safe place to live—a place where their children can grow up. They are looking for opportunities to express self-worth. They are as selfish and self-centered as any other generation. They fight existing situations in order to improve their living conditions. However, the good of the world is not their major concern. Young couples are not going to make over existing social ills and clean up the environment. But they are going to make a difference when they discover something amiss in their own environment. Their concern about other peoples' situations has yet to be demonstrated.

Children

"We decided to have one child, no more. The decision was based on what we want to do with our own lives. Both of us are professionals and intend to keep working. We want to give our child a quality life and recognize the limits of time we face."

"We didn't have any reserve when we got married and our parents are not well enough off to help us get started. So we both worked. We need to keep working. But we want some children. We decided to have one child and I cut back to part time. I like part-time work, and we are looking toward our next child."

"We were both nearly twenty-six when we got married. We agreed to wait four years before having a child. We wanted to get acquainted with each other and establish life as a couple before having a child. Then, we decided to have three children. We've planned a couple of years between each. It's worked out well."

"We had intended to wait a while before having children, but it didn't work out that way. Our first child came within a year. I've had to quit work, and it's been really rough financially. It's a good thing our parents are close by. They help out a lot."

These comments point up important characteristics of young couples: they plan their children, they want to have a life of their own, they are aware of the financial implications of childbearing, and they are waiting longer both to get married and to have children. These characteristics have been pointed out earlier. Young couples genuinely believe they can juggle several life-changing changes without failure.

Surveys and studies support their contentions. For instance, a survey of families indicates that women are going to continue to work regardless of the presence of children at home.[8] They, as one of the women above mentioned, may have to work because of need or, as another one said, because both want to pursue a career. No matter what the reason, women will continue to work while child care is handled by agencies or individuals who are paid.

As a result of such decisions by many young couples, child care has become a growth industry and has been so for a relatively short time. In previous generations when women had to work, child care was done as a convenience by relatives or neighbors. They were paid, but child care was not a big business.

Young couples are the propelling force behind the child-care industry. They want and need its services and products. As a consequence, child-care businesses include such diverse elements as training courses for natural childbirth, exercise classes for returning the body to prebirth shape, convenience baby-care products, and prenursery day-care centers. Young couples have influenced the industry by demanding quality products and care. They are serious about providing a good life for their children as well as pursuing their own life goals.

Their seriousness about children illustrates their penchant for quality. However, this desire may have negative results in the long term. They seem to want so much for and from children that they are bound to be disappointed when their children turn out to be average. Another negative aspect of young couples' attitudes toward children is inadvertent neglect because the parents want to continue to be themselves without assuming proper parental roles.[9]

On the other hand, they do have children even if at a later age than previous generations. They are not neglectful in planning for children—they just put birth off. Delaying childbirth is not unusual.[10] Neither is it extraordinary for a couple to wait three years between the first and second child. An indicator of birth planning is that the fertility rate was higher in 1983 than in 1981 for women between twenty-five and thirty-four. Couples are getting married later and are postponing children.

Another statistic relates to unmarried couples and children. Nearly 10 percent of couples with children had one child before marriage. The implications of such data are: (1) couples who desire children may postpone marriage even while having a child, and (2) children are born to couples who do not want them and who do not effectively use contraceptives. In any event, some couples with children are not necessarily married.

Children, however, cause major disruptions in some couples' lives.[11] Having established an equilibrium between themselves, a couple plans for a child. It arrives, and they discover they are not prepared for the consequent demands of the child or for the feeling of being tied down. These feelings are especially difficult for young couples who have been accustomed to traveling and engaging in various leisure pursuits. They will need assistance in making the transition from childless to parenting couples.

Technology

It is no happenstance that home computers were created by people between twenty and thirty-four. This is the technological generation; they have been immersed in technology since childhood. This immersion may have begun with their parents who saw some of the old Buck

Rogers comic strips. Because young couples have watched the launching of a space ship, a rocket streaking to the moon, a man walking on the moon, have participated in supersonic travel, and seen robots on TV and the movies, they are not afraid of technology but enjoy and use it.

A review of presidential campaigns illustrates how the media has changed the methods and procedures for getting votes.[12] In the forefront of this change have been the young pollsters. They are the visible elements of the young couples we are discussing. Using techniques and methods they know excite their peers, they suggest multi-media events for advertising products and showing off celebrities. It is the generation of technologists—young couples—who are changing the way we think, feel, and imagine.

Even though this generation bought fuel-conserving autos during the energy crisis, they upgrade to more sporty models when the opportunity arises. They are seeking an image. The word *image* itself bespeaks technology. An image is created, polished, and presented via sophisticated marketing procedures. This group knows the value of technology.

They will have to be technology-minded because this is the age of computers and computer-dependent gadgets. Satellite communications and electronic mail are common. These methods of handling communications have been invented because young people, especially those between twenty and thirty-four, have the money to purchase and an interest in using new technological products.

This group uses computers a great deal. They want computers and computer education to become a part of the curricula in schools so their children will be "computer literate." They use computers at work. Many work in their homes and use computers to hook up with offices. These people are intense—their lives are associated with chip products and processes.

In spite of their easy rapport with technology, this generation is concerned about technology's effect on people. Naisbitt's suggestion that personally written messages is one way to counteract impersonal technology is important. Young couples want to take advantage of technology, but they are as selective with it as with other forms of life-pattern changes. Young people should not be written off as having no concern for individuals or feelings. It's just that expressing this concern in a manner understandable to older people is sometimes a problem.

Summary

Young couples are concerned with issues and problems unrelated to specific generations. However, they approach those problems and issues, and express those concerns in a manner quite different from older adults. In addition to this difference in attack, young couples have a sense of self-confidence bordering on brash disregard for the opinions and experiences of older couples. They are aggressive and outspoken.

No wonder older folks have difficulty understanding and working with young couples. They represent a new age. Yet, there are continuities between their parents and themselves. Values are similar. Young people are better off financially than older folks were at the same life juncture and are listening to their parents about enjoying life while they can. They want a good life and are willing to fight to change conditions that they feel inhibit their life's quality. They are waiting to get married, are planning when to have children, are willing to upset tradition when it conflicts with their aspirations, and are comfortable in a technological world.

Few of these are attributes of older people, who while they may have learned tolerance, can take only so much brashness and questioning. They feel young people need to respect their experience. These older people like to be listened to and are not accustomed to younger people being equal to them. Older people don't like conflict and can't handle it well. They don't trust computers, and many are repulsed by the images on television. Young and old apparently live in two worlds.

Reconciling these worlds through the church can be an exciting and rewarding experience. It is to this task of joining older and younger couples in ministry that we now turn.

CHAPTER FOUR

An
Approach to
Ministry
❧

W e don't want you to tell us what to do. We can figure that out. We need to have an approach, a way to start. Give us some ideas; we'll do the rest."

"Our people are interested in a ministry to young couples but every time we've tried something, the couples don't come. We know we need to get them in, but as a group they're almost impossible to program for."

"We have a good young couples' group. They're active and alive. They ruffle a lot of feathers sometimes by what they say and what they do. It takes a lot of my time to smooth things over, but they make a vital contribution to our church."

These pastors convey the mixed feelings many congregations have about a ministry to young couples. These couples are needed, and congregations are interested in creating a place for them. Yet, it is hard to attract young couples, and programming for them is unusually difficult. Attitudes often cause this stand-off.

Young couples' attitudes do make them hard to work with occasionally. They are not wholly to blame for a congregation's problems in starting a young couples' ministry, however. Attitudes of older members can make the development of such a ministry unnecessarily difficult. Older people conveniently forget the world is different from the world they lived in when they were younger. A hard-line emphasis on discipline and deferred gratification may have been appropriate two or three decades ago, but it must be reconsidered in today's social climate. At the very least, discipline and hard work ought to be redefined.

Another source of friction between older and younger couples is a result of the image of life given by older people. Young couples have been eager students. Not only have they heard the admonitions of their parents, but they have acted on them, too. Older people who don't like what young couples represent should take part of the blame. After all, young people were trained to be independent, critical, and aggressive. Older people are also responsible for providing an affluent setting—young people have become used to a good quality in life because their parents provided them with one.

It is regrettable when conflict mars the initiation of a young couples' ministry. Antagonism between younger and older couples doesn't bode well for the future. Indeed, casting stones at each other is not a good beginning for a ministry. An effective ministry occurs because people are committed to an ideal and work together to move their congregation nearer to the ideal. They accept differences in approach and understanding as normal aspects of life. They are resilient; if one strategy fails, they try something else. Unfortunately, beginnings and failures cause conflict. When conflict is not resolved it creates a chasm across which a bridge of understanding is hard to construct. This happened in at least one of the congregations previously mentioned.

Quite a different situation was apparent in another of the congregations. This congregation's goal was strengthening the church's mission, and the members were successful as long as that goal governed their activities, with the pastor acting as an interpreter and stimulant.

In the third situation the pastor was very specific about the need his congregation had for a young couples' ministry. This congregation had leadership, training potential, and the finances necessary for creating a ministry with young couples. What the members lacked was a strategy they could test and use.

Such strategies are critical. These are methods a congregation uses and tests as it approaches or starts a new ministry. Proposed strategies are based on planning; they can be developed and followed by rote. However, this kind of strategy encourages failure because it allows little or no deviation from the plan. There is another kind of strategy that encourages testing. Such a strategy, when it includes challenges to each new idea and proposal, encourages thinking.

I intend to construct a method for approaching a ministry with young couples, with the suggested approach designed to stimulate thinking rather than be adopted and used without modification. After all, a congregation should know or learn about the young couples its ministry seeks. The congregation, in addition, is in a position to test ministry ideas with leaders of young couples. Therefore, the emphasis in the following discussion is on adopting an approach to ministry rather than establishing a set of rules. Each congregation is responsible for adapting the approach based on its needs and the mission it seeks to accomplish.

A Theological Foundation

A ministry, regardless of its target group, rests on a perception of God and an understanding of how God's will is to be followed by a congregation. No one is enlightened enough to comprehend fully the magnitude of either God or God's will. Each of us, like Paul in his description of love, sees God dimly (I Cor. 13:12, RSV). We are entrusted with minds capable of delving into God's mysteries but are limited by procrastination and fear in our search for God's will. Yet, as Christians and as congregations, we must proclaim the grace and faith of God as illustrated in the life and teachings of Jesus.

A beginning point in developing a theology of ministry to young couples is separating cultural mores from God's commands. A society establishes an ethical basis, mores, governing relationships between people, and between people and things. Anthropological studies have noted the evolutionary understanding of these relationships through the millennia.[1] A perusal of anthropological studies reveals that humans often regard some of their conventions as godly commands. That's a danger with accepting cultural mores uncritically—then they take on the aura of holy dictates.

The basic Christian message is contained in Jesus' statements regarding the essentials of a committed life (Matt. 22:36-40, RSV). Jesus said putting God first and loving others as we love ourselves is the basis for ministry in God's name. Even though many interpretations of these commandments exist, they are the foundation of a theology for ministry to young couples.

Theology, in this context, does not discriminate between couples who are married, living together, or homosexual. However, societal conventions, upheld rigorously by most conservative religious persons, condemn homosexuality and do not openly condone unmarried couples. Conventions like these are essential because every society depends on sex to produce children and families to provide social stability. Codes of conduct surrounding sex, family units, and children are very important to societies. While these codes are not sacred, transgressing the codes is punishable in most societies.

This doesn't mean societies demand all sexual activity to be confined to spouses. Societies know there will be deviations and have special rules for exceptions, including prostitution and concubinage. In addition, homosexuality has been part of human history through the centuries. These kinds of conduct are aberrations of socially approved sexual codes. Society in general depends on conventional family units (as defined by and for each society) for sexual relations and stability.

Theology, however, is asexual. It focuses on relationships and commitment. It deals with sex and sexual partners as relationships that ought to express Christian love. This is quite different from the rationale behind societal conventions. Families are units in which Christianity is taught, learned, and expressed in intimate ways. Such units are not established solely to produce children or to ensure societal stability.

In spite of prevailing social conventions, God speaks to all varieties of couples. God's will may even be understood and advanced by couples who are not monogamous or married. A theology that limits God to a specific form of couple is culture-bound more than expressive of God's will.

A theology, in addition to being asexual, is community- or group-oriented. A Christian fellowship is composed of people voluntarily coming together to encourage, instruct, and lead each other in following the commands of God as these have been revealed in Christ. Jesus illustrated the viability of such a community. While his power came from following God as closely as possible, his influence was based on the enthusiasm and faith of a committed group. Jesus was preceded and followed in his travels by a group of believers who preached and taught. This group encouraged, instructed, and led each other after Jesus' death. God worked through them because they personified a spirit. A theology that doesn't emphasize a committed community of believers is without worth.

A congregation interested in developing a ministry to young couples must have an asexual theology. The marital status of young couples is not an issue in creating or sustaining such a ministry. The primary concern should be assisting people in finding commitment to God. A second concern should be to encourage and instruct those people in expressing love to each other and to others they encounter every day.

A congregation's theology must focus on winning people rather than setting obstacles or boundaries. Jesus' emphasis was always on winning people to God, not asking them to forsake something else. By his manner he demonstrated that God's way will lead to a more fulfilling life than is possible by following some other teaching. A congregation without this emphasis is not preaching in the fashion of Jesus.

When this emphasis on the better way—Jesus' way—becomes the central focus of a ministry, young couples will be attracted. If the theme of a ministry to young couples is to "give up," "be like us," or "these are the rules," it is likely the ministry will fail. That's how important theology is to a ministry. A congregation must understand that God calls people and takes them in whatever condition they might be. It is not a prerogative of a congregation to add hurdles to the call so people cannot hear it and thus not be able to heed it.

An effective ministry begins with theology. A congregation intent upon having a young couples' ministry must decide which of its ideas about ministry are *cultural conventions* and which are *interpretations of God's will*. This decision will provoke an interesting, if painful, discussion. Once concluded, the discussion will need to be revived regularly so a facade of intentions does not stifle growth in understanding God's intent for humans.

Creating an Approach to Ministry

A strategy for accomplishing a task is based on data and careful planning. Data have been presented earlier that can be used to assist in developing a viable strategy. However, we must analyze and interpret those data in order to fashion a workable approach to a ministry for young couples. Two essentials to strategy development are purposeful intention and change. Once these are in place, a strategy that relies on collected and analyzed information can be constructed to create a ministry.

Adjusting a generalized strategy to the needs of a specific congregation will take additional work. An approach to ministry for a particular church depends on acquiring, analyzing, and interpreting local (community and church) data. Information, primarily about attitudes and life patterns, will come from young couples. Similar data, as well as perceptions of ministry, will be collected from congregational leaders and members. Adapting a general strategy to the needs of a congregation then will be relatively straightforward. However, intention and change must be discussed before building even a general strategy.

Purposeful Intention

No church program of consequence just happens. Good programs are the result of planning, effort, and timing. And planning is being intentional. Selecting leaders, training them, discovering and acquiring resources, finding a place for meetings, and undergirding the program with financial support are aspects of careful planning. None of these can be slighted if a ministry is to be designed and implemented.

The most crucial element in developing a ministry for young couples is deciding to do it and then doing it. Procrastination is a fatal disease. Tomorrow never quite gets here, and those good ideas and hopes remain as dreams and ambitions. Young couples grow older and, if the church doesn't act now, will find other institutions to invest their time, energy, and money in. If it puts off until tomorrow the initiation of a young couples' ministry, a church will have lost an opportunity to influence not only them but their children.

Being purposeful means work. A ministry is not created by voting in favor of the idea at a church's governing board meeting. Such a vote is one of confidence rather than one of action. In reality, much effort should have been expended prior to considering the idea of a young couples' ministry at a board meeting. Goals of the congregation should have been established, data on the number of potential young couples should have been collected, conversations with nearby congregations that have ministries for young couples should have been held, and commitments from the pastor, some lay leaders, and one or two young couples to act as organizers of the ministry should have been completed before any vote by a governing board is taken. Creating a ministry is indeed hard work. It also demands time and effort from a variety of people. When the scope of this activity is understood, it becomes clear that a congregation must act on its desire to have a ministry for young couples.

The congregation signals its intent to minister with young couples by setting this program as a church goal. If the ministry is to be created, the goal should have a three-year minimum for making it operational.[2] This will allow time for collecting background information about the need and potential for the young couples' ministry. Additionally, a three-year time span will allow church leaders to carefully cultivate prospects, select and train leadership, and have at least one year for actual programming. The beginning point, however, is setting the goal. That's the first sign of action.

The next step is actively collecting information about the number of young couples in the church or reachable by the church.[3] These data are available from church records and pastors who visit. Community data can be secured through the schools.[4] Parents of children through third grade would normally qualify as young couples.

With data in hand, the pastor, a lay leader or two, and one or two young couples can begin assessing the possibilities of creating a ministry. One or two informal conversations within this group might lead to an informal gathering of a group of young couples. The intent of these meetings is to measure the degree of interest in creating a young couples' group, getting ideas about the types of programs that might be attractive, and ascertaining the kinds of support needed from the congregation. It is well to remember that exploratory conversations generate expectations. If a congregation is not willing to follow up on those expectations, no meetings should be held.

The next step—following up data collection about the potential for and interest in such a ministry—is to recruit some leaders and set aside time from a pastor's workload for this ministry. A ministry needs attention and cultivation. Individuals must chisel time from other commitments in order to help create a new ministry or to make an existing one more effective.

The number of people who respond to efforts at recruitment and asking for time will determine whether or not a ministry can be started. Candid acknowledgment of time requirements, for example, five meetings during the next six months, must be made to each person chosen to serve on the leadership team. The persons who agree to serve should be aware also that their efforts will result in a new ministry by the congregation.

The next step is to hold some meetings for young couples. This is the program in action. This comes after much work and planning have been done to develop an interesting program.

A final step is evaluating the program and the ministry in light of the purpose of the congregation and its goal of ministry. Evaluations should be annual, involving members of the governing body of the church as well as leaders and participants in the ministry.

These steps are measures of purposeful action. Without any one of them, the congregation will not be ready to minister to young couples. A church can decide not to proceed during or before any one of the steps. Deciding not to engage in a ministry is as intentional as choosing to initiate one.

When a church decides to have a ministry, it must change its habits. This need for change must be confronted and dealt with creatively.

Change Is Necessary

The path of least resistance is not to change. Of course, the world about us changes and forces us to adapt, but this is passive or cooperative rather than intentional and active change. A vital congregation is not passive. Initiating a ministry demands active change. Active change is following a plan and generating new habits. Both of these are critical when a ministry is begun.

Change without a purpose upsets churches and people. Planned change and purposeful programming can help people better utilize their gifts and responsibilities. Planned change is necessary when a ministry is created, as well as when a ministry is terminated. The key word is *planned*.

Plans are rooted in the past and accept the challenge of the future. They call us to uncomfortable situations because they force us to grow. A congregation without a plan for recruitment and growth, for instance, is headed for decline and decay. Without stimulation and conflict, a group doesn't bother to think about its future—it is content to exist and hope tomorrow will be like yesterday. But the concept of ministry is active and purposeful, depending upon planning. It continually seeks weaknesses in its approach to its environment and tries to be more effective in exemplifying its message to those it wants to reach.

The first change, then, is for a congregation to live by purposeful planning. The congregation not only must want to reach young couples, but it must change its way of thinking so it can create an approach to get to and attract them into the church's life. Many, if not most, churches play at planning. It is a rehash of what went on last year, or it is such a drastic departure from previous programming that people are confused and put off. Purposeful planning is sensitive to the need for continuity as well as challenge.

Initiating a new ministry ought to enhance the entire program of a congregation. In the case of a young couples' ministry, benefits should come to the children's education and music program, the adult education program, attendance and participation in worship. Members may be added to the choir, and the congregation may broaden its fellowship program. Unless the congregation is willing to make changes in each of these program areas, a ministry to young couples should not be attempted.

Specific changes will be required in the attitude of church members toward newcomers. Welcoming and making new persons feel at home are attributes of few congregations. Yet, these are vital to any program aimed at young couples.

Another change will be the way conflict is handled. Young couples can tolerate more conflict and can deal with it more directly than older folks. Unless older congregation members are willing to work out conflict on a more direct basis than they have in the past, a ministry to young couples shouldn't be started.

Training and incorporating new persons in leadership positions will demand changes from many congregations. Few churches have training classes for new leaders, and most congregations prefer to use "our kind of people" as leaders. This means they don't want leaders who are too aggressive or innovative. Young couples are the prototype of disturbing leadership for many churches. Older people will have to change their perception of good leadership or forgo a young couples' ministry.

This list of needed changes can be lengthened and made more specific by leaders in any church. The point has been made—habits must be broken and new ways of working must be adopted. That's the reason the word *purposeful* is used. Without a great deal of intention and perseverance, a congregation will not be emotionally prepared to deal with a young couples' ministry.

Program Elements

A ministry to young couples demands purposeful action and change from a congregation. This ministry requires, as well, inclusion of certain elements in its programming to ensure its viability and to maximize its contribution to the total ministry of the congregation. These elements are program-related but are very much a part of the approach to ministry. They are essential to the strategy guiding a young couples' ministry the same as purpose and planned change are.

1. *Intergenerational Interchange*

An adult education class on issues of concern to young couples was being led by a panel of three women. The oldest, in her late seventies, was making a point. "One of the things I've learned is that I needed to be less concerned about my child's development and more interested in enjoying life at whatever stage I'm in. I wish I'd known that when I was your age!"

A parent was talking to an about-to-be-mother. "Pay attention to your own health. Get away from the baby regularly. It'll do you both good. Don't feel guilty about going out with your husband or friends. If the baby is in good care, you don't have to keep yourself anxious."

Intergenerational insights and information help young couples retain a perspective on themselves and their problems. Older people can communicate their accumulated experience and learnings to young couples in informal conversations. When the church helps structure such interchange either in fellowship settings or in adult education courses, young couples can listen and learn without feeling defensive. This is not to imply young couples are incapable of helping older people learn. Education and fellowship are not age-bound. The context of the setting is a key to helpful exchange. The church can structure opportunities for mixing ages and experiences. The resulting interchange of ideas and information will be especially helpful to young couples.

Churches have discovered that forming interest groups is an especially good method for encouraging intergenerational interchange. Family night programs is a medium used to promote fellowship and sharing between various ages, including both parents and children. Family camping can be a good experience for young as well as older couples (and singles). Social action committees, counseling youth groups, and operating food pantries are other activities that bring together people of various ages. They not only come together to work at a common task, but their informal conversations as they get to know each other encourage sharing of experiences and learnings. The sharing benefits both old and young.

2. *Age Specific and Couples' Groups*

Most congregations have some form of couples' groups or clubs. Passing years have a way of blinding older people to the young people's need to belong to a special group just for themselves. Unnecessary and unintentional tensions are caused when young couples are invited to become members of the only existing couples' club in a congregation rather than being encouraged to start a new one. Young couples need a group of their own the same as older people need a group of peers for companionship and support.

It may be helpful in some churches for young couples to break into segments according to age categories. Young couples under twenty-five have different needs and ambitions than many of those nearing or just turning thirty. For instance, the experience level at work and ability to build relationships are distinct according to age group, even though the number of years don't seem that far apart. Also, the life goals of couples change after a few years of living together. Older young couples, those near or over thirty, may be more intent on settling down at a career or in a home than are couples who haven't reached twenty-five.

A major difference occurs in young couples when children arrive. Once a couple has a child, their life pattern, interests, and needs change considerably. They are confronted with an internal crisis, trying to reestablish equilibrium to their relationship while caring for a young child. Shortly, they become much more concerned with community and church matters. Their peers will increasingly be drawn from among other young couples with children. The friendships between young couples with children and those who are not parents will not cease, but the times they see each other will decrease dramatically.

A danger for most churches is in limiting their ministry to young couples with children. A vital couples' ministry will not focus only on parents and children. Many couples are waiting a few years before having a child. If the congregation decides not to program for them until they have a child, these young couples may decide the church isn't interested in them. They may drop out of the church or slip away from its influence. When this happens, the congregation may not be able to reach them. Couples need the church's program regardless of whether or not they have children. For this reason, no church should concentrate on one type of young couple exclusive of other types.

3. *Education and Social Programs*

A meeting schedule combining information and opportunities for fun and fellowship seems to be the best for young couples. They enjoy living and want to have a good time. Conversely, they are serious and seek self-improvement and self-fulfillment. A young couples' program that fails to provide both education and fellowship will wither and die.

By the same token, every program must be contemporary. That is, it must address issues from the perspective of young couples. Developing such programs may be trying for older adults, but people respond only to those activities speaking to their needs and concerns. Young couples are vital and self-centered. They are not content to be passive partakers of activities that do not call for their involvement.

Trying to find the right balance between education and social enjoyment is difficult, to say the least. Peers are important to young couples. Attending church school classes and belonging to fellowship groups are contingent upon who else attends and belongs. A young couples' group is similar to a youth group. The church attracts or repels friendship cliques. That's the reason it's necessary to tap into the interests and needs of young couples as their meeting schedule, including education and social fellowship events, is being developed.

At least three types of educational activities should be considered for young couples' programs. One type of education revolves around personal development. This includes such things as career advancement—advice related to getting along with people, with the boss, with a mate and so forth, and managing their lives as they relate to time use, methods for selecting which group or activity to participate in, and setting aside periods for physical fitness and personal growth. These kinds of courses will attract certain types of young couples, primarily those who are aggressive and oriented to executive or professional life patterns.

74

Another type of education involves the creation of a support group. This is the form most adult Sunday school classes take. The program theme might be Bible study, but the instructor should be wise enough to allow the group to move with its own agenda. The group's needs will revolve around issues they confront as individuals or as couples. The support and care they need will be found in the church school group.

A third kind of education is information given to couples who don't want to have a great deal of interaction with others. This is usually a lecture, the kind of presentation typical in some church school classes or talks at monthly meetings of a young couples' group. Anonymity is prized but so is the information. This kind of education usually is best when handling very personal or controversial subjects, such as child abuse, sexual relations, in-law relations, and the like. Information is given and ideas ignited, but interaction is limited to questions of fact or interpretation. While some young couples prefer to discuss these issues, many young couples are not secure enough as couples to handle such topics in a give-and-take manner. They prefer to hear an expert and then test their own perceptions in private.

Combinations of these types of educational events may be useful in some churches but not in every congregation. The nature of a young couples' ministry will determine which or how many of these kinds of educational activities will be used in a specific setting.

4. *Discussion*

Young couples like to talk and want to be heard. They want to discuss issues, particularly those items affecting their group life. Some young couples may be reticent to handle personal issues in a group, but nearly all of them will have an opinion about their group's life. They ought to be encouraged to discuss its purposes and goals as well as where its program should lead.

A discussion can be a meandering expression of various opinions, or it can be structured and purposeful. There are times when each form of discussion is important. The meandering type is especially useful when emotions are high and several topics need venting. A good leader will allow the discussion to move at its own speed and direction. The result of this kind of discussion will be to release feelings and to prepare for serious considerations at another meeting.

A structured discussion is issue-specific and certain results are expected. A planning meeting is a structured discussion. An educational session relating to parenting may be a structured discussion. A fellowship meeting may contain a structured discussion as part of a game. The topic of the structured discussion may be anything of interest or of concern to the group. It needn't result in an earthshaking decision. It is a form of group participation, moving people in a particular direction and accomplishing a specified purpose.

Young couples need to be aware of these two types of discussion and intentionally plan to use one or both of them in most meetings. Leaders will need to know which type of discussion is necessary for the program event they are planning. Skilled persons will need to be recruited to lead each discussion. Although young couples like to talk, they desire results. It is up to their leaders to help them talk and to have satisfactory outcomes to those conversations.

These four program elements are essential to planning vital young couples' programs. No matter what the size of a congregation is, it is possible to create an interesting and helpful program for young couples so long as these elements undergird the planning.

It is obvious that discovering and recruiting young couples through peer groups, understanding their needs and wants, working with them to create interesting programs, and training leaders to help guide the group's life take much work. A congregation wanting to have a ministry must affirm its decision through its efforts to create and sustain it. As the church will realize, the rewards of having such a ministry are significant. The keys to successfully initiating the ministry, however, are purpose and willingness to change.

This brings us to the reef on which many a good voyage has ended: irreconcilable differences of opinion and values between young couples and older folks. We need to think more about this problem before ending the discussion of an approach to a ministry with young couples.

Resolving Differences

"If we didn't do or say anything, there wouldn't be any problem. But we're not going to be quiet and let older people tell us what's good for us and our children. It's our lives, and we ought to have a say in how the church program affects us."

"We want young couples. We just don't want their aggressive ways and nasty comments. They're so pushy. We'd be glad to make changes, but not if they're going to keep on hollering at us."

A stalemate has been reached! Each of these comments represents a legitimate point of view. Each comment must be heard. But both speakers will need to change tone and attitude before any resolution of the issue can be found.

How to encourage those changes while protecting each individual is the issue for church leaders. I wish it was as simple as one, two, three, but it isn't. Some church disputes have a long history, especially in small congregations or churches with powerful or extended families. People remember each other's negative sides as well as they do the positive. An outcast at age five is still trying to be an insider at age twenty-five. Disagreements in the church often are not related to any program or activity it sponsors.

Regardless of its origin, a dispute that finds its way into the church must be handled there.

The first step in resolving differences is to pinpoint the one or two issues at the heart of the matter. Often this is a style issue—someone doesn't like the way another person recruits or trains or plans. Finding the cause takes time and patience. A lot of peripheral noise and emotions may be vented before the real obstacle emerges.

Helping groups slice through to the key issue should be done by an individual trusted by both sides. Sometimes this is the pastor, but often it is best left to an outside expert hired to help resolve the conflict. No matter who does the task, finding the problem is step one.

The next step is interpreting and explaining the positions of each group to the other. Not allowing emotions to control discussions is a major part of this step. Often, when people know the goals and hopes of each other they can begin to build the bridges necessary to cooperate. Explaining, understanding, and interpreting are important at this stage.

The next step is developing and getting each side to accept a compromise. No group is going to accept fully another group's philosophy and life pattern. Yet, several groups in the church can live and work together toward common purposes. Helping groups understand that tension shouldn't deter cooperation is important in this step.

The next step is pointing both parties to the goals of the church and helping them find ways to work together in accomplishing those goals. This will be hard to do, but within a year it is likely the relationships will be solid enough to withstand further conflict.

These four steps can be used no matter if there is a major conflict or if there is only a minor misunderstanding between groups. When older folks know some of the difficulties and desires of young couples, they will be more tolerant of their actions. When young couples understand the hopes and dreams of older folks, they will be more willing to tone down their rhetoric and be less adamant in their demands.

The pastor's role in maintaining harmony and understanding in a church cannot be overestimated. The pastor should make it her or his business to head off controversy and conflict. If this isn't possible, the pastor should be quick to find someone to help resolve the difficulties. As long as conflict is allowed to separate groups in the church, that's how long the church's mission and ministry are hampered.

One way to curtail misunderstanding and conflict is to merge young couples into positions of congregational leadership. This isn't as hard as it may seem. The next chapter outlines some expectations of young couples, which when taken seriously by church leaders will make their participation in congregational life easier and more beneficial to all parties.

CHAPTER FIVE

Involving
Young Couples
in Ministry
❧❧❧

T hey're always competing with each other. One tells a story, and the other tries to top it. I thought that kind of stuff happened only at work, but this is a church meeting of young couples. It isn't something we like to be involved with."

"Maybe we'd be more active if you let us help plan the programs. We would like to have a voice in what our group does."

"We're enthusiastic even though we don't know everything. Give us a chance to learn by doing."

"We don't like programs of the couples' groups. Why can't you let us experiment with some new approaches? Let us use our ideas. Don't sell us short."

Young couples want to be in charge. They have confidence they can fashion a group without equal. They have more energy and verve than older couples and are willing to expend it to accomplish their interests. They can get excited about experimenting with programs and group life. Yet, they can be difficult to get along with. Their ideas and aggressive attitudes not only can turn off older couples, but they sometimes have trouble getting along among themselves. Therefore, a congregation must be as aggressive as young couples and must have patience in working with them, too.

The comments above serve notice to congregations wanting to develop a young couples' group that to be effective it must work with them rather than for them or in their stead to start and keep the ministry going. A congregation cannot expect to create a young couples' ministry without committed involvement from at least some young couples. An organizing principle is young couples must participate in the creation of their ministry, or they have to be provided ways of feeling ownership in it before the ministry will be effective.

In spite of their aggressive and skeptical attitudes, any program young couples create must address their needs and interests. A typical shortcoming of church planning is that the group charged with this responsibility thinks it knows the problems and opportunities faced by the group. Unfortunately, planners often project personal issues into programs that should work on group problems. Any organizing committee of young couples needs sympathetic assistance from an older person before it can initiate programs and activities addressing their problems and opportunities.

As with every adult ministry of a congregation, those to be reached must create and maintain the group and its program. At the same time, an outsider's perspective is an important corrective to the narrowness a small group brings to program planning.

The necessity of uniting a specific ministry with the overall approach of a congregation emphasizes the congregation's stake in the program and in the group. The congregation should be involved through its own leaders, active support, and selective participation in each of its group's activities. However, each group within the congregation has a life of its own and must be given enough rein and freedom to make it viable. Responsibility of the group to the congregation should not be minimized, but a reciprocal relationship must exist. A congregation should not interfere with a group as long as the group's programs help the congregation accomplish its purpose and goals.

Many young couples the congregation wants to reach have not had a history of working in the church. They may be coming into a congregation after being inactive for several years. Consequently they are accustomed to business, school, or community but not church activities. They know office or workplace politics. They are uncertain about whether these kinds of procedures have a place in a congregation. They don't know how a church gets things accomplished. They must be acclimated and acquire competence in new roles. The congregation's need to enforce rules has to be tempered with patience and care for people who are unused to the church's setting. The congregation should be aware that young couples resist rules but tend to thrive on caring relationships.

Assisting them in making the transition from secular organizations into the world of the congregation may be frustrating at times, but it will have long-range benefits. Not only will young couples have the immediate role of setting up and sustaining a specific ministry, but their commitment to the church can grow as they assume leadership and support positions in other aspects of the church's life. However, the critical first step of preparation for ministry should not be lost on any congregation wishing to create a young couples' ministry.

Perhaps the most common mistake in the transition process is giving people too much to do with too little support and preparation. People are not taught to swim by being tossed into water and told to make it back to shore. They are given information, moved slowly into deeper water as they learn various strokes and floating techniques, and must pass tests before being allowed to go into the deep water. A parallel of learning to swim is helping young couples become involved in the church. These people, since they are being initiated into adult life and learning to live as a couple, need training in church life and leadership. They must not be overloaded with responsibilities. They can assimilate just so much at any time, and there are limits to anyone's energy regardless of age.

A more careful analysis of these factors can make it easier and more productive for many congregations to start and maintain a young couples' ministry. Every situation is unique. The particular situation will alter factors affecting the creation of a ministry and the amount of caution a congregation uses in dealing with young couples.

Involvement in Planning

"The planning process begins with general goals. The planning group takes these goals and narrows them down to one or two they feel can be accomplished. Then they work out the procedures for meeting the goals. Procedures include being specific about numbers, potential, and budget. When the procedures have been worked out, assignments are given to people to make certain things get done so the goals are met. An evaluation process is put in place so the planners can measure how well the goals are met."

This brief statement by the chairperson of a church committee condenses planning in the church. What he didn't say was that in most congregations a small group is responsible for both the planning and making the plan work. The only way burnout is avoided in planning groups is to keep recruiting new people every year so that work is shared. Depending on the same one or two couples for several years is a sure way to kill a program. They get tired and may become resistant to new ideas.

Saying that young couples must be involved in planning their own ministry and program doesn't mean they have total freedom. As with other ministries, they have to function within the context of a congregation's goals and procedures. Freedom to create a program carries limits. However, imposing a process that requires approval by a church governing body for specific events and programs will be detrimental and result in a stilted, unsatisfactory program.

On the other hand, it is possible for a program to be viewed differently by various congregation members. For example, a young couples' group may decide it wants to schedule three meetings led by a sex therapist. The idea of a sex therapist coming to talk could cause some older people to protest. They may argue this is not an appropriate activity for a church group. Such a limitation is unnecessary and improper. A program relating to relationships, including sexual aspects of relationships, is at the heart of Christian life. The context of the program—its Christian message—is what is important rather than the content in this instance.

Involving young couples in planning often requires congregations to reassess their procedures. For instance, the congregation just mentioned should stress limits as these relate to program context more than to program content. Its focus on program content should be to discuss life issues of its members and potential members rather than depending on past principles of acceptability to guide its planning. This illustration also suggests that anytime a congregation becomes serious about involving young couples in planning, the church had better be clear about its assumptions and planning. They cannot be treated differently and will insist on being given freedom to innovate within certain guidelines.

Second, to involve young couples in planning, a church should have specific overall goals. Planning a ministry to a particular group requires that the church knows what it is and where it wants to go with its program. Young couples are used to planning and are aware of planning contexts. They have been taught to plan in school from elementary years through their last day of formal education. They want to know the rules—in this case, what the church is about and how they are expected to fit into its overall scheme.

Third, a church must be willing to negotiate with young couples. Young couples have participated in political activities for most of their lives. They think some sort of political behavior must be part of church planning but may not know its subtleties. They are interested in using an acceptable political process to get their program legitimated. Unless a congregation is able to allow them to participate as equal partners, a ministry to young couples should not be attempted.

Young couples don't want to be manipulated by an unfair system. They want to trade off opportunities under a process allowing them good returns. When a church doesn't play fairly with them, they tend to lose interest and go elsewhere.

Fourth, evaluation is understood by young couples to be a normal part of planning. If a congregation insists on ignoring evaluation for all of its program while requiring it for a young couples' ministry, it is discriminating. Either make evaluation a part of planning for the entire congregation, or scrap it for everyone. Don't burden one aspect of a congregation's ministry without requiring the same for every other part.

Involving young couples in planning is one way to shape up a church's planning process. They may be young, but they are probably more experienced in planning than most older members, as they use planning in their lives to a greater extent than others. It is essential to plan and every group functioning as a part of a church's ministry must be represented in the planning process. When young couples are involved, planning takes on new meaning and importance.

Long-term Values

"I've heard and said the younger generation isn't value-grounded. After working with them for a few years, I have to eat my words. They have the same basic values as their parents, but they express those values in modern terms. The world has changed drastically over the past three decades and how values are lived out has changed too."

"Could you be more specific? Give me a 'for instance.' "

"Well. Raising children is a value. I was taught that children were important and should take center stage in my life. Their welfare was my primary concern. Young couples value children, but they also know that they themselves are just as important as children. The values spotlight is no longer focused only on children, but it shines across the spectrum of human life. One set of values may not be emphasized so much, because others have been found to be just as important."

"Perhaps. But what about Christian values? Do young couples support them as much as in the past?"

"That's a hard question. We don't know how to measure a person's allegiance to Christian values because these values are lived out in many small ways each day. We put a lot of reliance on church attendance and membership figures because we think this gauges a person's Christian values. Perhaps these statistics tell us something, but I'm not convinced they are indicative of how well we live by Christian values. And, I'm as convinced as ever that the proportion of people living by Christian values is about the same now as in previous generations. I can't prove that, but neither can it be disproved."

This conversation between a teacher and an interviewer illustrates how hard it is to determine the expression of

Christian values in a population. It is not so difficult, however, to demonstrate that people who are supported in a particular form of behavior will tend to continue behaving that way. The success of rehabilitation programs for alcoholics and weight watchers depends upon support groups for behavior modification. The principle of encouraging a certain form of thought and behavior has been an important part of the church's life since it began. It is the foundation of known religions.

One of the primary reasons for creating a ministry for young couples is to assist them in identifying and incorporating Christian values into their lives. A support group where participants can help each other test ideas about values and how they are expressed in daily life is an important goal behind establishing any ministry by a church. Young couples, because of their importance to the life of a congregation and because of their vulnerability to many new, conflicting pressures, are an especially critical target group for most churches. They are the future of society and, in many ways, represent the future of the church. If the church is to pass its Christian values on to the next generations, it must work with young couples.

A ministry to young couples is not an option for a congregation—it is a fact. At some time every congregation faces its own demise. Leaders suddenly become aware of their age and loss of energy. They begin to understand how important it is to get a new generation involved or there will be no church. Then, and only then for some churches, they realize the need for a young couples' ministry.

For those churches who are interested not just in their survival but in ministering, creating a young couples' ministry is a normal part of church programming. These congregations realize that values are transmitted not solely by teaching but by creating groups to support a certain way of life. It is the group that helps convey and sustain Christian values over the long term. That's another reason for having a young couples' ministry as part of a church's total ministry. The congregation can serve as an additional support group for young couples as they cope with expressing Christian values in their lives.

The fact that a young couples' ministry creates a two-way learning and support situation within a congregation counters the argument that "We're starting this ministry for them." A ministry is reciprocal. It does as much for the sponsor as it does for the participants. A congregation is obligated, by definition, to express Christian values. The manner in which these are expressed may change over time. Changing the methods for expressing them is generally dependent upon feedback from younger generations. As they teach, they also learn. This applies to both the congregation and the young couples' group.

Young couples are not going to assimilate and practice Christian values without help. It is too hard emotionally and spiritually to function in isolation from others. A young couples' ministry is essential for young couples to grow in the image and manner of Christ. A ministry can assist them to identify and incorporate Christian values for their long-term life.

Learning by Doing

Adults learn best by doing. They need some information to get them started on the right track. Once they receive the information, they need a chance to put into operation those things they have heard. This is the theory behind the apprentice concept, whereby most craft trade unions train novices through apprenticeship programs.

Craft unions have programs for training new people because they recognize the need. Churches, for some reason, assume people are trained when they come to participate or are chosen as leaders. Few congregations teach members how to be Christians.

Groups (especially support groups formed according to age or marital status) often have events or monthly meetings where information is shared about some aspect of living. Unless this information is specifically about Christian living, chances are church members will not receive any training about how to express Christian values in life. An apprenticeship Christian program isn't available in most churches. That's the problem underlying the following complaint.

"You make us learn by the 'cold turkey' method. We are thrust into the middle of something and told to make it go. You don't tell us what you expect, give us an overall plan, indicate what kinds of support we will get, or let us know about a date for stopping. I don't think that's a fair way to use people in the church."

This young adult was telling the pastor about reality. It isn't fair or helpful for the church not to provide opportunities to learn by doing. It doesn't require much imagination or experimentation to set up chances for young couples to learn how to lead, to become aware of congregational goals, to try their hand at planning, or to know what the congregation expects. Unfortunately, most congregations don't have enough insight or interest in training to provide these opportunities. It seems that churches have not discovered that people can't learn by doing unless they are given opportunities.

Young couples won't know how to develop a ministry within the setting of a congregation until they are required to do it. They will need to be given much support by experienced church leaders as well as by the pastor. They need not be pushed to go faster than they feel they can move. They must be stimulated to want to continue even though results are slim at the beginning. In whatever phase they are in, they are learning. It is up to the church to make certain the lessons are learned.

In no way should failure be ignored or glossed over. Being positive about failing is to put the problem into a larger context. Learning happens when a failure is explained in a positive fashion. Of course, a failing is not a positive experience but occurs when results do not measure up to expectations. No matter if it is a monthly meeting, a planning session, or a recruitment drive, when any of these falls short of goals, they are considered failures.

Analyzing reasons for failing can be helpful to any ministry, including one for young couples. Some reasons for not getting expected results include not being thorough in planning, choosing the wrong people to be leaders, designing programs that look good on paper but don't speak to young couples, and setting a time when young couples cannot attend either planning sessions or meetings. Each of these can be remedied. Usually a failure can be changed when the reasons are identified and discussed. This means alternative procedures will be used in the future to alleviate the possibility of additional failures.

It is important to give adults opportunities to learn, to help them analyze both failures and successes, and to let them do their own programming. Congregations wishing to encourage young couples to participate in a ministry have to find ways to help them learn how to be good participants by letting them do the planning and leading for themselves. While this seems self-evident, many congregations stifle young couples from trying anything on their own.

Overload

Church leaders keep giving a few people more jobs rather than finding others to do some work because it's easier to depend on a few than recruit and train others. This happens in a young couples' ministry when church leaders or the pastor selects a small cadre—one or two couples— who become responsible for all the planning and doing of the ministry. They are in charge of recruiting members, planning meetings and events, securing leaders for the events as well as for the group, and setting the agenda for every meeting.

While it is obvious to an outsider that such a regime tramples on the good will and energy of this small ministry, church leaders ignore warning signs. Then they are surprised when members of the cadre drop out. People who are overloaded get tired and are unable to keep going at the pace required to keep a ministry alive.

A discovery made in researching types of ministry leadership is the reluctance persons who are coming into the church for the first time have in accepting any responsibility for total church programming. They do not feel competent to handle large jobs, nor are they comfortable enough with the language and requirements of congregational life to lead or even to participate. Long-time church members perceive their reticence as signs of disinterest and standoffishness. It may look as though young couples have no desire to get involved. These may be actual reasons for some young couples, but the main obstacles are they feel uncomfortable and hesitant. They are outsiders and must learn proper behavior before becoming too involved.

A new person on the block, in the apartment house, or at work is introduced to responsibilities carefully and gradually. This same technique should be used in the church with young couples. They ought to be assimilated slowly and carefully rather than be expected to become active immediately in all phases of church life.

Young couples may unintentionally deceive church leaders into thinking they are more willing than they actually are to assume responsibility. Because of their aggressiveness and ambition, they seem to clamor for assignments and jobs. However, they can do just so much by themselves.

Many young couples prefer to work alone rather than with other young couples. Others are petrified to try something without being part of a larger group. The result of the mixed signals young couples give to church leaders is that young couples may receive tasks for which they are unsuited either technically or emotionally. Just because a couple volunteers to do something doesn't mean they should be given responsibility for that task.

A misunderstanding of the social setting for a job may result in overload. Knowing the ground rules and the expectations is crucial for effective work in a ministry. When a couple is taken out of their familiar surroundings and asked to work in the church, they need assistance in handling their assignment.

This is illustrated by the experience of one congregation trying to start a young couples' ministry. The pastor was excited by a live-wire couple who volunteered to head up the publicity and recruitment campaign. They seemed to be naturals for the tasks as both had backgrounds in advertising, and each had been active in earlier days in churches. He eagerly asked them to go ahead and stood back because he didn't want to interfere. They failed miserably. They didn't meet deadlines; their suggestions for publicity were tepid; and they didn't contact any potential couple to ask them to become members. Within three months, they not only quit their job but stopped attending church.

The pastor was astonished. He went to visit them to find out what had happened because he felt partially responsible. The main problem, as he pieced it together from several conversations, was that the couple was used to give and take from others as they designed advertising campaigns. They were accustomed to specific budget figures to work with, and they had no experience at all in personal contact advertising. Their most important contribution at the start was their enthusiasm.

The pastor, who had been very high on this couple, changed his tactics for recruiting other young couple leaders. He resolved that (1) no young couple would be given responsibilities without at least one and probably two other young couples to help them; (2) each young couple who was asked to do a job would meet with him prior to beginning the task to discuss the church's experiences and expectations for that job; and (3) he or another church leader would meet with them to assist in planning. He had overloaded one young couple with responsibility, but he wasn't going to do that again if he could help it.

This pastor learned the hard way that being overloaded is more than the number of jobs people are asked to do. Overloads occur when the tasks are in unfamiliar terrain and no one clues you in as to how to read the environment. Sensitivity to overload includes training and support for each couple asked to do a job.

Another form of overload occurs when a job is not clearly specified; no guidelines are presented; a terminal date is omitted; and no reports are requested. A ministry isn't started or maintained in a vacuum. It is part of a congregation's total life. As such, it should be treated as any other growing thing. It should have goals, schedules, evaluations, accomplishment steps, and an overseer. When none of these are available for each assigned responsibility, the ministry is likely to flounder. People need structures. If a church doesn't establish an organizational process for its ministries, the failure rate for its attempts will be high.

A third form of overload happens when a young couple is asked to perform two completely different jobs. The overload occurs when the requirements for each job have no overlap with each other either in time or in interest. For instance, a young couple may be asked to serve as members of the schedule committee for their group and to be members of the senior citizens housing committee of the church. Some couples could handle these assignments, but the two sets of responsibilities do conflict. They may have little or no interest in coping with senior citizen housing—in fact, they never think about this issue at all. They would be better off as youth counselors where some of their experience may be useful.

Overload is another way of saying: Don't overwhelm young couples with jobs they can't handle, don't know the parameters for, and have little interest in. It would be nice if every young couple knew their limits. For example, in one congregation, a young couple consciously limits their jobs to one per year in the church. The wife has discovered through painful experience that she can handle successfully just one task per year. Church leaders who are sensitive to her limits have made her contribution to the church very effective.

Most people aren't that careful. They keep saying yes without realizing the bind they are getting into. It is up to the pastor or recruiter to spread the net wider and get more people. Knowing your people and their limits is a prerequisite for those trying to assign jobs and recruit leaders for a young couples' ministry. If you aren't aware of their needs for support and training, you can lose them. Being insensitive is unexcusable for church leaders.

Allowing Innovation and Discovery

A minister was commenting on a sudden increase in young couples in the church. "We sat down to look for the cause. We discovered it was because we had so many different groups they could be involved in. They weren't confined to a single group but could pick and choose."

That congregation was relatively large, but such a ministry should not be dismissed because of size. Young couples come to church because there are opportunities for them to innovate and to learn by discovery. Each generation must test the knowledge given them. Young people resist being told, but they understand experience. Having chances to be part of groups that are encouraged to learn by discovering for themselves is a key to successful young couples' ministries.

Innovation may be nothing more than using a different form of leadership, such as shared positions. This may be a practice used in several congregations but may be an innovative experience for some young couples learning to share responsibility and authority in the church. A congregation allowing this kind of experimentation will help young couples learn to be innovative.

Planning meetings that deal with controversial issues may be another form of innovation. Some congregations will not be able to handle the newness of such meetings. However, innovating through programs that address social and personal problems from a Christian perspective ought to enrich congregational life. This kind of innovation should be welcomed not only for what it does for the young couples but for its contribution to the fabric of the church.

Innovation may take the form of recruitment. A young couples' ministry may seek out those in the community who are unlike church members. Young couples may want to recruit those of different social, racial, and ethnic backgrounds. They may want to encourage nonmarried couples and homosexuals to become part of the young couples' program. These innovations can be difficult for a congregation. On the other hand, people in need of a ministry should not be rejected just because they "aren't our kind." If a young couples' ministry can break traditional barriers, it needs to be commended rather than condemned.

Learning occurs by discovery. Most new ideas are not original. Their newness depends upon who thought of them and the situation in which they are tried. Encouraging young couples to innovate gives them opportunities to discover through experience in a Christian environment.

For instance, sociologists and psychologists can illustrate the proclivity of people of particular backgrounds, races, and ethnic origins to want to be with others of the same type. Young couples may be able to break those barriers but in so doing come to recognize that the separations still exist on certain kinds of issues and practices. They learn safe grounds for communicating and participating with each other in the church. They discover areas (protected turf) that only people of the same background, race, or ethnic origin can tread.

Assisting young couples to learn and innovate will enhance not only their ministry as a group but will enlarge the outreach of the congregation. Letting young couples stimulate others and encouraging them to try different ways to express the Christian message will help the congregation keep alive.

Summary

Most of this chapter's suggestions can be used in any adult program by a church. Yet, young couples are special. They need to be involved in planning and leading their own programs. By the same token, they need guidance, support, freedom, and assistance from older and more experienced church leaders. These needs cannot be rationalized. By their nature, young couples need involvement in planning and leading. Older adults consider planning and desiring to be leaders useful to their programs but do not have the same needs in these areas as younger couples.

The church, however, is not for young couples alone. They represent one segment, although a very important one, of the church's total outreach and mission. Even if a congregation tries its best to help young couples with their program, one additional caution needs to be observed. Young couples must understand they are one part of a congregation's total ministry. How that is accomplished is our next concern.

CHAPTER SIX

Young Couples' Part in a Church's Ministry
❦

A ministry can be defined as "giving service, care, or aid."[1] A church's ministry is giving service, care, and aid to people in the name of Christ. Since there is a multiplicity of types of service, care, and aid needed by people, a church uses different tactics to meet those needs. Thus, a congregation's ministry is divided into parts, each of which gives service, care, and aid to a particular group.

Educational activities are one form of service and aid. Counseling is both aid and care. Fellowship events provide service, care, or aid, according to the kind of event and the needs of the individuals present. Young couples' groups are supposed to give care and aid to young couples and help them perform service in the name of Christ.

A congregation is a multifaceted attempt to minister to its members, community, and the larger society. How this is accomplished depends upon the commitment and energy of a church.

In describing a ministry with young couples, I have focused on one aspect of a church's program. My microscopic analysis must not confuse church leaders into thinking this is the only part of the total ministry of a congregation needing attention. It is one part. As suggested in the last chapter, each part of a church's ministry must be placed in perspective. It must be surrounded and supported by a total ministry before it can achieve its goal of effective ministry to a certain kind of member/constituent.

The primary reason churches engage in ministry to age, marital, or interest groups is to make its efforts at service, care, and aid be amenable to the needs of various types of people. If everyone felt comfortable working as a unit and had identical needs, no breakdown into program areas would be necessary. This isn't the case. People are different. They are age-specific—that is, they have special concerns according to their age and life situation. They have differing backgrounds, which influence their behavior and interest patterns. Thus, a congregation wanting to reach either a particular group or a wide range of groups will have to form ministries for the kinds of people they want to attract.

Creating a ministry for young couples is an outreach decision of a congregation. The reasons for making that choice were presented in the first three chapters. Briefly, the primary reasons are: there are many young couples in society; most of them drop out of the church's sphere sometime between high school and thirty-five; and the church needs this group. These are three compelling arguments for starting a young couples' ministry.

But these aren't the only valid points used to support the creation of such a ministry. Young couples need the nurture of the church as they develop life goals and test values. They need the support of Christian friends—fellow travelers—as they confront issues common to any Christian living in this society. In addition to gaining from the church through an organized ministry, young couples can help older Christians retain an edge to their commitment by challenging their comfortable habits and entrenched thought patterns. A ministry to young couples can be a mutual learning opportunity for congregations and young couples. Both can profit, and the church's witness and outreach can be enhanced.

A problem facing a congregation that turns its attention to a particular program is trying to keep the leaders of that program from thinking it is the entire program of the church. Youth may feel they need all the attention and support of the church. Church school leaders may think their efforts require all the church's support. A women's or a men's group may think their programs are the most important activities in the church. While it is essential to divide the church's efforts into various compartments, this separation is a danger. Each part may end up fighting against the other parts.

A unified church program is critical if any part of it is to be effective. Paul talked about this in terms of the body. He pointed out how different parts work together to make the whole (Rom. 12:4-8; I Cor. 12:4-31, RSV). A congregation is effective in its ministry when each part of its program is working for the same goals. A young couples' ministry will not be an outreach of the congregation until the church knows what outreach means and should do for those it touches.

After having said this, I still must maintain that ministry to young couples is different from most other church programs. They have to know where they fit in the church's life, but their involvement is crucial for the long-term vitality of a congregation. The caution of having an overall plan and approach of the church is not minimized in the following discussion. Rather, the necessity of having overarching goals is emphasized. Young couples must be shown how they fit into congregational goals so they can help achieve them in the name of Christ.

The uniqueness of a ministry to young couples must be reiterated. Identifying their place in the total ministry underscores the urgency of creating a ministry *for* and *with* young couples.

They Are the Future

A professor walking across a campus stopped to survey the students who were lounging on the grass listening to music, gathering in small groups to talk, and walking. She shook her head and muttered, "If these are the future leaders, we're in trouble."

An executive, after a weekly conference with the young people on her staff, was talking to a peer. She said: "That was the most selfish, arrogant bunch of newcomers I've seen. They think they're the boss around here. What happened to authority? Don't they understand business organizations?"

Her peer shook his head. "It seems like for the last ten years new staff members have been increasingly hard to get along with. They talk back, raise questions, and fight over almost everything. Some days I'd sure like to go back a few years when being boss meant being in control." He smiled and continued. "It was peaceful but not nearly as interesting. They're hard to get along with, but they're creative, sharp, and hard working."

The executive nodded. "I agree with that. I guess the problem I face is being complacent. They're telling us that the world is different today than it was when we dreamed about being boss. They think they can do a better job than we're doing. They give us the challenge and I, for one, am not going to let some young whiz kid beat me at my job!"

Two friends were discussing their children. "How's your daughter? She isn't expecting yet, is she? I heard a rumor the other day."

"Not only is she not expecting, but she told us the other day not to be surprised if they don't ever have any children. She and Bob want to spend a few years overseas as teachers. She has a degree, and Bob is trained in construction work. They are negotiating with the State Department to hook on with the development unit in some country."

Young couples are diverse in interest, education, and expectations. Yet, they are the future. They may not personify the hoped-for world of older folks, but they are going to have a lot to do with the shape of that world. Young couples, in a few years, will be the leaders and supporters of educational systems in local, state, and national situations; they will be strategists and operators of business and government; and they will do volunteer work in and manage organizations whose functions oversee and guarantee the welfare of millions of people. In every respect, they are the future.

Young couples are the future of the church as well as in other parts of society. No matter how different from past generations they may appear, these young people will take over the church. Those congregations that make it a point of antagonizing and isolating young couples will have to revise their ways. It makes no difference how unlike the present members young couples may be—they will be the church in the future. That's the way life works.

What are some implications of the future if this is the group that's going to lead? First, the values of the past will be those of the future. Continuity of values has been verified in studies cited earlier.

Second, conflict and conflict resolution will be more evident. Being heard and taken seriously is important for young couples. Church meeting and planning sessions will not be easy for older people. Young couples question procedures and aggressively seek programs especially for themselves and their offspring.

Third, an emphasis on quality may not materialize. It is difficult for members of a group to each be heard and get a part of their agenda accepted, at the same time focusing on quality. Democracy and consensus depend on accepting an agreed-upon standard. Such an agreement will not be top quality but will be closer to average. This means the general level of future church programming and meetings will not be much changed from the present.

Fourth, expressions of concern will be more pronounced than they have been in the past. This does not imply the future will focus on more people. Rather the concern will be upon the kinds of help the church gives to those who attend. In one sense, the church may become more narrow unless older people can train young couples in the meaning of outreach.

The future will be interesting for churches willing to acknowledge the importance of young couples. Those churches will develop the intergenerational learning and training opportunities essential to dialogue and joint planning. They will find ways to listen and hear young couples at the same time they are opening channels to talk with them. They will forge methods of handling conflict that eventuate in constructive negotiations.

The point is that while young couples are the future, they must grow into that future. Older people are going to be around for quite a while. Building bridges and planning programs jointly must begin, so transitions can be made easily rather than abruptly. Saying that young couples are the future of the church is a fact. However, they and older church members are obligated to work together to shape that future. Such joint efforts are impossible until young couples are in the church and accept it as an important organization. If for no other reason, this is important enough to cause a church to begin a young couples' ministry.

Their Children

Not every young couple will have children. This should be recognized. A young couples' ministry ought to be designed to accommodate those with children and those couples without.

Many young couples will have children and by their very nature, young couples will look to the church to find a place for their children. This place may be in a church-sponsored nursery school, in a Sunday morning education program, in a music program, in drama and art programs, or in a worship experience in which children are present. Once children arrive, a young couple's interest begins to focus on what's available for those children.

Congregations interested in ministry to young couples may find children a convenient recruiting tool. Some churches believe that getting their children involved may be an entree to young couples. This is harder than it appears, however. One problem is competition.

During the past decade, a plethora of service agencies has sprung up designed to work with children. Many of these agencies are concerned with working parents, but in communities where young couples' ministries are effective, churches compete well with these agencies by sponsoring nursery schools.

Another tactic of effective young couples' ministries is sponsoring a "mother's day out." This is a program where young mothers can leave their children at the church between specified hours on a given day and be free to spend that day on themselves. This concept is not new, but it fits the life patterns and expectations of young couples. They want to remain individuals and not be tied down by children every hour of every day. This program, in which they agree to give some time, allows them time off. Such a program has worked well in churches in diverse communities. Besides, the program is usually not based on paying but participating.

Christian education programs for children and youth are very important to young couples. They recognize the importance of education and also the need people have of relating to life goals and purposes. A church that works at training its teachers, using good curricula, and incorporating music and drama into education will be in a position to work effectively with young couples. Again, the size of the congregation is not critical. The need is for programs and leaders who care for young people.

For a church to ignore certain age groups of children can diminish, if not kill, the desire of young couples to participate in a church. This is especially true if a church doesn't provide a nursery for young parents. Lack of nursery care may also hinder young mothers who would like to participate in daytime events at the church.

A congregation interested in young couples must program for their children. If the children can't find a place, the parents will not be there either.

This raises another point about a young couples' ministry. A church can benefit greatly from having a babysitters' network. The aim of the network is to have people available for young couples who want to attend group meetings. It may be that most young couples in a community have relatives who will babysit while they go to the church, but this isn't true in many urban and suburban communities. In such situations, establishing a network may mean the difference between having or not having a viable young couples' ministry.

Ministering to a New Society

The church has persisted through the ages because it has found ways to minister to each emerging society. Young couples can be an important link in ministry to the society currently emerging in the world. They can translate the language of the church into the vernacular of the populace. They can identify the hurts people are feeling, and develop strategies and remedies for healing those hurts. They can isolate issues that cause conflict and devise methods for handling those issues in a creative, consolidating manner. Young couples can be the group primarily responsible for assisting a church minister in a new age.

They will not do the ministering by themselves. That's the reason it is important for every church to have overall goals and purposes. Young couples can point out problems and issues and then work with other groups in the congregation to address those issues. Young couples can be partners in mission to the new society; in fact, because of their insights they may be the frontline missioners to the society. However, they cannot do the job alone. They need the entire church behind them.

Why can't older people minister to the new society without the help of young couples? They can if they feel in tune with the ethos of the emerging society. However, many older people are uncomfortable in a technologically oriented age. They don't like computers, view robots with fear and skepticism, and regard telecommunications as too future-oriented for them. They might use all of these at work, but older people don't appreciate what these inventions represent as a new way of life.

Nothing but their attitudes and interests prohibits people over thirty-five from ministering to the society represented by those between twenty and thirty-five. They aren't stopped by factors out of their control. People over thirty-five tend to be more concerned with issues they are dealing with than with those confronting others. Their energies are used in solving their problems rather than in giving time to assist those younger than they. Older people have gone through those ages and continue to move into new vistas themselves. They need to be brought back to the needs of young couples before they can give any attention to their needs. Young couples can help them remember. Young couples also can persuade older people to use their experience in training young couples to become witnessing Christians in the emerging society.

There really is no beginning or ending to a society. Societies evolve unless a cataclysmic event occurs. Such an event is always possible, but in the normal course of history, societies are continually changing. *Emerging society* means changing modes of expression and conduct. New mores are fashioned by each generation. Young couples have helped shape the mores and conduct codes acceptable to them and their peers. They need to teach older people the meaning of these new patterns of life.

As previously pointed out, values underlying the changing society tend to be constant. Expressing those values is where change is most noticeable. Young couples can explain the differences and help develop strategies to effectively reach members of the new society. An assumption underlying this cooperative attitude is that the church is reaching young couples and involving them in a meaningful ministry.

Innovating and Experimenting

"Let's be mavericks. Let's do something different this year. Everything has been so structured and sterile this past year. We need to innovate!"

The female member of a planning group was asking for the chance to be different even though she was a part of an ongoing program. She wasn't as dissatisfied as she sounded. Her complaint was the committee seemed to be on the verge of doing the same things it had done the previous two years. She wanted other people to realize that to change wasn't a sin.

Few people, especially young children, like an unsettled environment. Structure is the name of the game. When people reach the "responsible years" between thirty-five and fifty-five, they tend to want to keep things steady. They are at a point in their lives when even the slightest change could produce unwelcome results. They are enmeshed in a career or job; they have seniority, which usually moves them up on the income scales; and they have children to raise or child support to pay. They are at the peak years of dependency—everyone seems to depend on them.

The responsible years inhibit people from experimenting. They can't afford the risks. They must have a stable life pattern that cuts down on their personal and familial stress. That's one reason they appear to be such traditionalists. They have to set an example and revert back to rather rigid adherence to values they grew up with. They are willing to allow younger people to innovate and to experiment and may silently applaud the successes of younger innovators. But they aren't in an emotional or financial position to take the risks of innovating and experimentation themselves.

Unfortunately, not many persons over thirty-five are ready to verbalize their feeling of being limited in innovating. But they are limited. This means that innovation and experimentation is left to those who have less to lose, either those younger or those older. Since change and innovation are emphases of young people, most experimentation and innovation in the church become their activities. Young couples fit into this category and should be regarded by churches as one group that can help test new models for ministry.

Experimentation and innovation presuppose an existing base. One innovates by adjusting or changing a procedure or process. One experiments by adding or subtracting something from an existing procedure or process. In discussing innovation and experimentation in the church, it is important to understand the assumption that changes are being made to current programs. The result may be additional activities or new groups, but the base is what now exists.

This means young couples are guided in innovating and experimenting. They are working within a tradition and an organization. They do not have a free hand to overturn or throw out what now is functioning. They can add to it, change its direction, or redeploy assets to better fit current needs. As with everything in life, limits must be observed.

Yet, young couples must be empowered to experiment and change. The church grows in strength and outreach as it tries different approaches and techniques. Older people may counter young people's suggestions with, "We tried that and it didn't work." They are entitled to their opinions. Times and conditions change. What didn't work a few years ago might be just the ticket for today. Allowing young couples to think and try is a prerequisite for a congregation interested in ministering to today's world.

An Interpretative Buffer

Agents who effectively implement change have an organizational insider who interprets the need for change to one group and cautions the person initiating change about going too fast. A young person getting ready to tell her parents about her boyfriend becomes the buffer between him and them. She is the go-between and is forced to interpret actions of both to the other.

A young couples' ministry must have someone to act as an interpreter to the congregation. The need is not to placate older people but to link young couples to the other parts of the church's ministry. Older people have more tolerance for change than is evident. All they ask is for change to be consistent with existing programs. They don't require carbon copies of activities but want the content of programs to reflect their church's mission.

The word *buffer* might offend some people. It suggests the advisability of having someone in a position of authority—an elected official of the congregation, the pastor, or a respected layperson—who can cool off language and emotions when conflicts erupt. The term buffer implies resilience and understanding. In addition, the individual must show concern for several points of view as expressed by both pro and con elements.

A church wishing to initiate a young couples' ministry should establish a *court of appeal*—either a formal one or else appoint someone to be an "ombudsperson." Any time new language and customs are introduced into an existing organization, some people will be disturbed. A buffer or court of appeal can help explain and interpret to critics and proponents alike the advisability of modifying an approach or correcting a direction. These persons are particularly helpful when a young couples' ministry calls in a controversial speaker or plans an event not considered tasteful by other congregation members.

Being a buffer is not a passive job. The buffer is active and functions with the overall goals and purpose of the church in mind. No one or no group should be able to influence the buffer to a great degree. In order to function well, the person ought to have the blessings and support of the pastor and the governing body of the congregation. Without those sources of authority, an individual would be unable to perform the interpretative task well.

Another form of buffer is shared information. Letting the congregation know about long-term goals and group meeting plans helps them gain a perspective on any ministry. Questions raised because of one activity may be answered if those raising the queries knew how this activity fits into the long-range plans of a group. Conversely, the congregation should share its procedures, goals, and activity schedule with a young couples' group. The aim of sharing by both groups is to keep each other aware of activities and to emphasize that both are working within the congregation to accomplish its goals.

Older People

Much has been said about older people in this book. Most of the time the reference has been to the next older generation, those between thirty-five and fifty-five years of age. The older people are of the same ages as the parents of the young couples who will be recruited for a ministry in any congregation. This older group has definite views about how to begin life as a couple, about parenting, and about working in the church. They will share their opinions, even to the point of intimidating some of the young couples.

Yet, these older people are supportive of much of what young couples want to do. They recognize themselves from a few years ago and see their children in the attitudes and actions of young couples. They may not like specific activities but may grant young couples the right to learn for themselves. On the other hand, they may not be willing to relinquish leadership positions and may make unreasonable demands on young couples. That's the reason for having a buffer. He or she can interpret activities and calm fears.

There's another group of older people, those over sixty, who tend to relate well to many young couples. They are of grandparent ages and know that their leadership and support days in the church are numbered. They often envision young couples as a way of ensuring the life of the church that they have sacrificed and worked for over the years. They are not saddened by their own loss but support the need for young couples to take over and have their day in the sun.

An alliance with this group may surprise some young couples. They view old people as uninterested in them and their views. These young couples forget that once those older folks were their age, with many of the hopes and ambitions young couples are wont to express. Age has not diminished their hopes but has rechanneled them. The dreams must be passed on to and carried by young couples. That's part of the rationale behind support from the over-sixty group.

A ministry to young couples completes a cycle for older people. They have had their chance and did the best they could. Now they are willing to give the reins to another group with energy and ambition. They are not ready to forgo their own responsibility and leadership, but they share it with a new generation. That's one of the promises of a young couples' ministry. In fact, coming full circle and beginning again is the way the church keeps itself alive. God continues to call people, young couples and others. Older people don't want current leaders to cause young couples to miss that call.

Summary

This book presents data to help church leaders better understand the needs and potentials of young couples. A theological statement focusing on the demands of Jesus to "feed my sheep" regardless of the type of couple is included to stimulate thought and provide a basis for an effective ministry. Finally, suggestions are given as to how a ministry to young couples ought to be implemented and its need for a special niche in the overall congregational plan. The one thing yet to be done is for the congregation to consider its total ministry in light of the need to work more effectively with this important group.

Each church must determine whether to accept the need for and whether it wants to try to establish a ministry to and with young couples. As it engages in its discussions, each church should realize that its potential as a Christ image for a certain group hinges upon its decision about a young couples' ministry. The future of the church is people—young people and children. Both of these elements, essential to a congregation's future, are assured by an effective ministry to young couples.

CHAPTER SEVEN

Illustrative
Program
Ideas
❦

Young couples are looking for ways they can be useful while finding self-fulfillment in the church. They also want the best kinds of church programs possible for their children.

The following program illustrations come from churches of various sizes. These congregations have found that programs for young couples work best when their leaders are trained, inspired, and supported by the pastor. This is not to burden pastors with additional jobs but is a recognition of the great influence a leader's personality has upon young couples. The pastor's attitude toward young couples will turn them on or off to the church.

Four types of programs are used to illustrate program ideas. Each type includes some specific programs taken from congregations across the country.

Adult Education

An adult education program for young couples should: (1) train some of them to become leaders in the church and (2) involve them in developing programs from a Christian perspective. In addition, the congregation should support young couples' programs by supplying resources and encouragement.

1. *Young Couples' Class*

This is a traditional approach to ministry for a new generation. It works! A larger congregation in the South, in order to keep this class specifically for young couples, put an age limit on its participants. Their rule is that the combined ages of the couple may be no more than seventy. This means that by their mid-thirties a couple moves to another more mature couples' class. This church has found that an impersonal cutoff point relieves a feeling of being picked on.

The class enforces its rule by holding an annual recognition dinner for those who have been a part of the class but are moving to the next age level. This is a good send-off. This process assures the young couples' class of not aging and forces it to reach out to new people.

A young couples' class becomes a friendship and support group for those who belong. A danger is that it will limit its membership by becoming an "in" group. This is avoided or minimized in a southwestern congregation that insists on rotating all leaders who are connected with developing programs. This tenure rule is applied to church school classes, in addition to other church offices.

The young couples' class, in congregations where it is effective, receives the same kind of support given to other adult education classes. This is through teacher training, resource materials, notices in the bulletin and newsletter about their program and special events, and having a couple as members on the adult education committee.

2. *Special Interest Classes*

Some congregations, like one in Indiana with a young couples' class, plan one or two special classes each year for those who want to work on a specific issue. The type of special class varies from year to year. One class may be for newly married couples and deal with forming a Christian partnership in marriage. Another special class proven popular is on disciplining your child. A third important class has been on managing a household in which both spouses work.

A special interest class is limited in time. It may be four or six weeks but should not be longer than two months. Young couples like the support that comes from their regular class. The special interest class is much more intense and focused than the regular class. Some congregations have found that one special course a year for young couples is sufficient.

The special interest class is in addition to the regular young couples' class, supplementing a particular segment of the existing class, and some young couples will not want to attend it.

Leaders for special interest classes emerge from the young couples' program in an upper Midwest congregation. Sometimes the leader is a young couple, and in other instances leaders are friends or work companions of young couples. This congregation has found short-term classes to be an excellent way to train new leaders.

Young couples should be in charge of planning their special interest classes, as well as the content of their ongoing education program. Most congregations have the pastor or the education committee chairperson as part of the young couples' planning group to ensure a strong relationship with the total adult education program of the church.

3. *Multi-course Education Program*

A few congregations, like the one in Ohio, plan monthly classes for adults. They have an annual curriculum of thirty to thirty-five courses. This congregation makes certain at least one of the courses each month is geared to the interests of young couples. This church depends on young couples' fellowship groups to care for their nurturing and support.

This church insists that at least one young couple is on the planning committee of the adult education program. This principle ensures that during their year-long series of programs, there are several addressing the needs and interests of young couples.

Youth Programs

Young couples are eager to support their children. They encourage their children to participate in church and community youth programs. A church youth program, then, is an opportune way of involving young couples in the church.

Young parents may become support or backup groups for youth. For instance, a choir program for young children in a southern church enrolls parents to sort music, to be substitute choir directors, to take care of robes, and to be in charge of refreshments once a month. These parents have become a support group for their choir children.

Young parents may use their talents to train, coach, and teach children and youth as is done in a church in the Northeast. Young couples in this congregation have been backstage crew members for youth dramatic productions, voice coaches for youth soloists, teachers in special youth programs, and organizers for youth-sponsored dinners and programs. Many of these young couples have been brought into the church because the church reached out to them for help with youth.

Young couples, by their nature, want to be active. They are not going to be content to do as they are told. They must be part of the planning, as well as the implementation of a youth program. By the same token, they should be thanked for their efforts. While this may seem like a common

115

courtesy, young couples are sensitive to being slighted or not recognized for their efforts.

1. *Choirs*

Congregations of every size have a few children who could sing if they were encouraged to and had a leader. In a western congregation, two young couples wanted a church choir for their children. In cooperation with the choir director, they initiated a children's choir. It had five members to begin with and, several years later, its predecessor has six members. Meanwhile, other young couples have taken over the organizing and the support group functions.

As this illustration points out, one or two young couples, given encouragement and support, can start a children's or a youth choir. The congregation benefits from their singing at worship occasionally or on a more regular basis. Although the number of voices may be small and their professionalism limited, children and youth choirs are among the most appreciated forms of youth programs.

2. *Bell Choirs*

In one medium-sized congregation, a children's and a youth bell choir are the products of young couples' interest. The young couples are part of the adult bell choir and decided to start a program for children and youth. One parent is the director. Young couples are asked to help transport the equipment when the choir goes to another church to perform. In addition, the young couples form a support group for adding to the number of bells and having periodic parties for bell choir members.

3. *Dramatics*

One congregation of about three hundred members has a young couple who trains youth as members of the stage crew in dramatic productions at Christmas and in the spring. This couple handles staging, lights, backdrops, and electronics. The result of their training is youth who can assist other groups in the church with sound and lighting requirements for regular or special programs.

A congregation in the Southwest regularly recruits young couples to be dramatic coaches and producers. Every other year the congregation has a play or musical for children and youth. The production is chosen and staged by young couples.

A small congregation in the Midwest produces one play each year using a combination of young couples, youth, and children. In some years the leads are adults, while in other productions the youth are the main characters.

Another midwestern congregation uses plays adapted or written by members, several of whom have been young couples. These are mostly children's plays. The choir director adapts the music for plays if needed.

4. *Trips*

Young couples, parents mostly, are chaperones and drivers for youth trips in many congregations. A southern congregation has discovered that its young couples welcome the opportunity to take a few days off with young people. Each year the youth take some sort of trip. They may go to an amusement park, to the beach, to a camp, or on a tour with a youth choir. In each instance the young couples who go along pay their own way. They are selected because of their interest in youth or because of needed experience as nurse or stage crew coach.

5. *Work and Study Projects*

Young couples have interests that may be translated into youth work or study projects. One small congregation had young couples who organized youth to work with another church in the community in creating and stocking a food pantry. Young couples in a large church in the Southwest recruited and directed youth in a clean-up project in a neighboring community after a major storm. A young couple in a tiny community in the South got four youth to give a week helping a community group repair the home of an aged resident.

The variety of work and study projects for youth seem to be limited only by the imagination and time of young couples. When young couples are encouraged to become actively involved in youth programs, their interest increases the chance that youth groups will help others through work programs.

In addition to the types of youth programs cited, young couples have been trained as youth counselors in many congregations. When they have the training, the support of the pastor, and good resources, they do an outstanding job. They seem to have a better feel for youth needs than do older parents. In addition, they have more energy to participate in some of the more active youth events, like games, car washes, and work days.

Fellowship Groups

Young couples need fellowship. They like small groups. Those congregations with growing young couples' groups make certain there are fellowship groups just for them within the church's program.

It makes sense, as a large urban church has demonstrated over the years, to separate young couples into small groups. These have been structured around age, around young parents, and interest groups such as educators, business people, and the like. In order for the smaller groups to feel part of the whole, regular events are scheduled to encourage young couples to meet others outside their primary friendship and interest group.

All church events are planned to bring young couples into contact with other members. These events, in a northeastern congregation, are planned around the Fall Fair, Lent, and Spring Homecoming. Everyone is involved in planning and working for these events. The work and fellowship surrounding the events draw young couples into the church. This congregation has used these church events as a means for increasing their leadership and expanding their program. Young couples have been a target of their efforts.

An unwritten rule for young couples' groups is that participation is not limited to church members. A southwestern congregation, which insisted that its program was for members only, lost its young couples' program. Visitors felt pressured to join the church. Young couples don't respond to such pressure, and before long another church in the community had a large young couples' program. The difference between the two churches was on requiring membership before participation.

1. *Different Groups*

A large midwestern church was having trouble attracting young couples. Its members were getting older. Using a bold strategy, this church allowed its young couples' group to divide even though it was relatively small. The members wanted to separate along age lines, parents and nonparents, and couples with teenagers and those with elementary children. This seemed foolish to church leaders, but they were desperate. Within a year the program had mushroomed. Young couples were attracted to the church because they could affiliate with a fellowship group with needs similar to theirs. In this case, separation assured a revitalized congregation.

2. *Young Parents*

A West Coast congregation initiated a young parents' group separate from other young couples. It discovered

119

that the group attracted young couples mostly under thirty years of age, whose first child was preschool age. It found that these young couples, as soon as the child got into some kind of school, moved into the other young couples' group. In this congregation, the special focus on young parents had the effect of an entree for young couples who might not have been attracted.

3. *Working Parents*

A small church in the Southeast looked carefully at its membership and noted the large number of working parents among its young couples. This congregation decided to focus on this group by forming a fellowship program. The response was tentative at the beginning because several young couples thought it was just another night out. Church leaders persisted and got three young couples to take over the planning and leadership. Within a year a good program was underway. The church leaders figure that half of their young couples are involved in the program at least three times a year. This is a success from their point of view. In addition, some of the young couples have become leaders in other aspects of the church's programs.

4. *Interest Groups*

Some churches, like the one in a midwestern city, define interest groups according to occupation. Their young couples may choose from among business, education, art, music, dramatics, and social issues. As might be expected, their young couples tend to be affluent and well-educated.

Most congregations do not have such a focus. They are more like the church in the Northeast, which uses an annual fair as a means for creating interest groups among young couples. These interest groups are workers for the fair. The groups may include woodworking, arts and crafts, quilting, cooking, and others. Young couples are attracted because of their interest, hobby, or desire to learn. Each interest group meets to work and to have fellowship in informal situations. The fair is a great success, as are the young couples' interest groups.

Special Needs

A few types of ministry to young couples might be done ecumenically or by more than one congregation. Ministry to couples experiencing a divorce, to those with children with serious birth defects, to those who are seriously injured because of an accident or natural disaster may involve more than one congregation—especially if the church has a small membership.

Several congregations have picked children with disabilities as a program focus. This is a special ministry of a midwestern church where a young couples' group had a couple whose first child had a serious birth defect. This group rallied around the young couple and looked around the community. The young couples were astonished to find that several other young couples had children with serious deformities or problems. This young couples' group asked for and received permission and support to establish a special ministry to young couples with children suffering serious birth defects.

The intent of this ministry is to bring together young couples with children who have special medical or psychological problems. These young couples become a support group for each other. Their program usually consists of medical personnel or social service agency representatives who discuss advances in treatments or available benefits. Because neither the congregation nor the community is large, this program includes young couples from several churches. It is supplemental and does not replace young couples' fellowship programs in the congregation of each young couple.

An especially difficult ministry is the one in which a young parent or a child suffers from a terminal disease. Often, a congregation tends to provide a special ministry through an existing young couples' group as happened in a church in a small community in the lower Mississippi Valley. A young mother was diagnosed as having terminal cancer. There were two small children. The young couples' class, which functioned as a learning and fellowship group for this church, decided it needed to show its concern to the family. The young couples' group helped this family through two years of continuing crises. During the first year the mother died. During the second year, the young couples helped settle the father and two children into a new living pattern. The feeling of love and care in the congregation grew tremendously. Helping was never an easy task, however. Taking care of meals and laundry were only two of the jobs these young couples assumed.

Summary of Program Ideas

Illustrative program ideas have been shared in the areas of adult education, youth, fellowship, and special needs. Each program was developed because the church leaders felt a need to involve more young couples. Each program was planned in cooperation with and led by young couples. These programs did not take the place of or overshadow similar activities for older couples, nor did they exclude programs for single individuals. However, the congregations involved, after initiating the additional programs, discovered much interest among young couples in their church.

Concluding Thoughts

A church's ministry takes place in a social world of continual change. As a result, pastors and congregations are constantly struggling to align their groups, their activities, and their services, so as to satisfy the needs of new generations of members. This book has addressed the needs, difficulties, and opportunities of work with one specific group—young couples.

In fact, this group is very important because young couples will take over the church. Their offspring will be the children and youth in their church school, and the young couples themselves will become the church's leaders. Their understanding of the church and its mission greatly depends upon how older church leaders and the pastor instruct, train, and involve them in ministry while they are still young couples.

Those churches willing to reach out will discover that young couples are adept at many things, but they cannot be thrust into church leadership and responsibility without first learning about goals and purpose in ministry.

A church's ministry is a living and growing process; a heritage is not passed on without change from generation to generation. Each new generation must make that heritage a part of its own life pattern. In so doing, the focus of ministry tends to shift somewhat, so that the newcomers can use their own words, images, and meanings to explain and expand their missions.

Older persons may resist these changes, not because older people are rigid, but because they want to defend what has taken them years to build. Therefore, linking the new group with older persons in a common framework for ministry is a necessity for churches wishing to develop an effective young couples' ministry.

A ministry targeted for young couples needs to be kept in perspective. Such a ministry must support the mission of the church and be part of the congregation's outreach. It has to have autonomy within the framework of the goals and purposes of the church. It needs freedom (within guidelines) to experiment and to design its own programs. It needs support and official recognition. It needs a recruitment program, and its leaders ought to receive training.

Each of these needs has been discussed. My hope is that congregations will understand how urgent it is for them to seek out and work with this very important population segment. Young couples are not only the adult children of older church people, but are the future church, as well.